A Treasury of Nature

ILLUSTRATED POETRY, PROSE, AND PRAISE

Leland Ryken

© 2024 by Leland Ryken

All rights reserved. No part of this book may be reproduced, stored in a retrieval system, or transmitted in any form or by any means—electronic, mechanical, photocopy, recording, or otherwise—except for brief quotations for the purpose of review or comment, without the prior permission of the publisher, P&R Publishing Company, P.O. Box 817, Phillipsburg, New Jersey 08865-0817.

Unless otherwise indicated, Scripture quotations are from the ESV® Bible (The Holy Bible, English Standard Version®), copyright © 2001 by Crossway, a publishing ministry of Good News Publishers. Used by permission. All rights reserved.

The Scripture quotation marked (NASB) is taken from the (NASB®) New American Standard Bible®, Copyright © 1960, 1971, 1977, 1995 by The Lockman Foundation. Used by permission. All rights reserved. www.lockman.org

The Scripture quotation marked (NCV) is taken from the New Century Version®. Copyright © 2005 by Thomas Nelson. Used by permission. All rights reserved.

Italics within Scripture quotations indicate emphasis added.

Some Scripture texts presented in the literary readings have been reformatted.

Some of the explications within this volume incorporate material from Leland Ryken's previous titles *40 Favorite Hymns on the Christian Life*; *40 Favorite Hymns of the Christian Faith*; and *A Treasury of Thanksgiving*—all of which are published by P&R Publishing.

Cover art is taken from Jean-Baptiste-Camille Corot (1796–1875), *The Eel Gatherers*, 1860/1865, oil on canvas. Courtesy of the National Gallery of Art, Washington, DC. www.nga.gov.

Printed in the United States of America

Library of Congress Cataloging-in-Publication Data

Names: Ryken, Leland, editor.
Title: A treasury of nature : illustrated poetry, prose, and praise / Leland Ryken.
Description: Phillipsburg, New Jersey : P&R Publishing, 2024. | Includes index. | Summary: "Calvin, Spurgeon, and Luther appear alongside Wordsworth, Twain, and Emerson in a vibrant celebration of God's creation. Ryken joins great works of poetry, hymnody, prose, and art with accessible literary analysis"-- Provided by publisher.
Identifiers: LCCN 2024010252 | ISBN 9798887790305 (paperback) | ISBN 9798887790312 (epub)
Subjects: LCSH: Nature--Literary collections. | Christian literature. | LCGFT: Poetry. | Hymn texts. | Creative nonfiction.
Classification: LCC PN6071.N3 T74 2024 | DDC 820.8/036--dc23/eng/20240326
LC record available at https://lccn.loc.gov/2024010252

Dedicated to readers of my books
over the past half century

Vincent van Gogh, *Oleanders*, ca. 1888

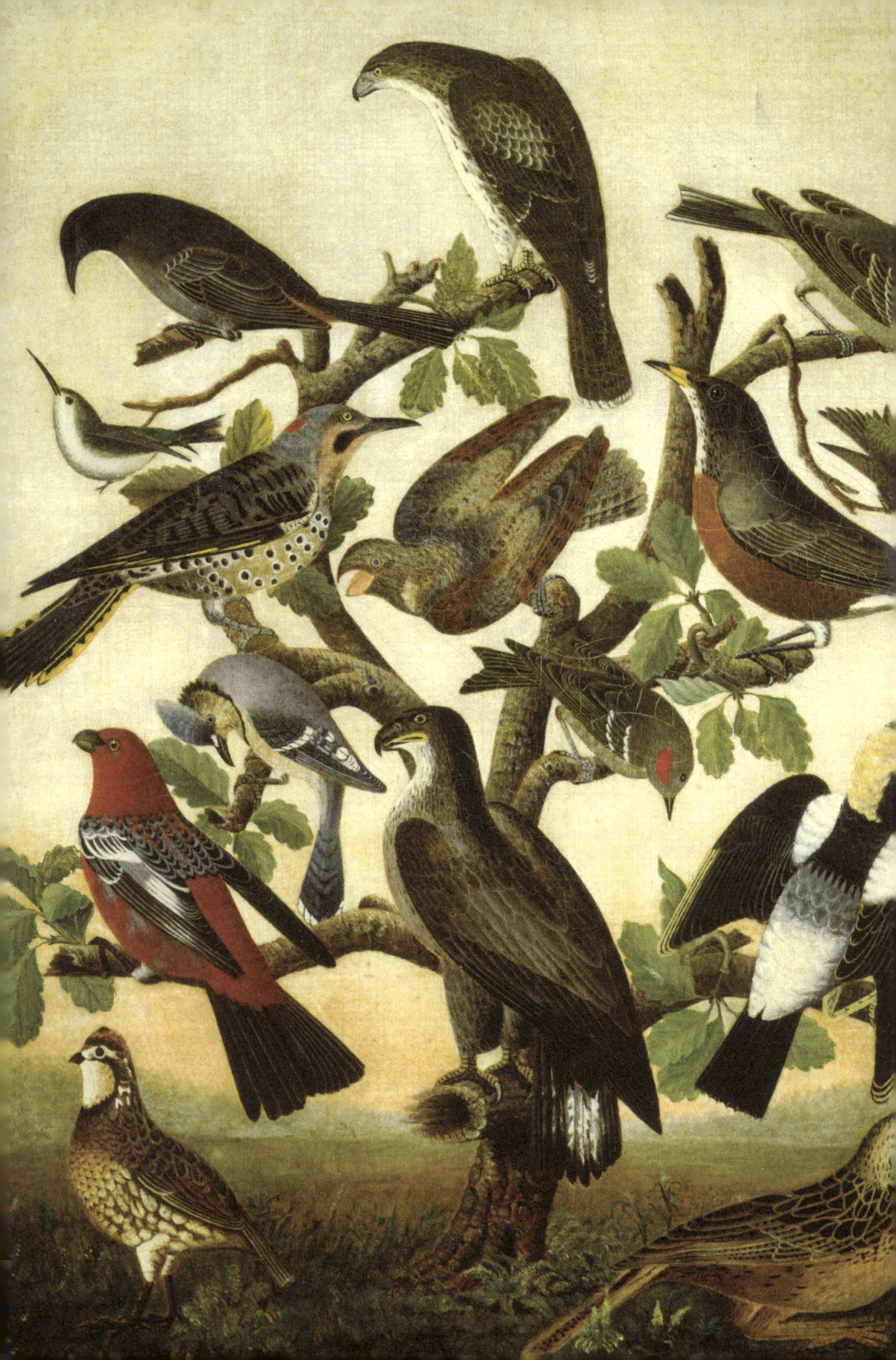

Contents

Introduction   9

God Visits the Earth | *Psalm 65:5–13*   15

God's Presence in Nature | *Martin Luther*   18

Canticle of the Creatures | *Francis of Assisi*   22

For the Beauty of the Earth | *Folliott S. Pierpoint*   25

It Is the First Mild Day of March | *William Wordsworth*   28

Prayers about Nature | *Book of Common Prayer*   32

The Theater of God's Glory | *John Calvin*   36

Famous Hymns Inspired by Nature | *Augustus Toplady, Henry Van Dyke, and Annie Hawks*   40

The Sun Also Rises, and the Sun Goes Down | *William Wordsworth*   43

Jesus' Command to Imitate Nature | *Matthew 6:25–34*   46

The Rhodora | *Ralph Waldo Emerson*   50

Where Shall Beauty Be Found? | *Edgar Allan Poe and Jonathan Edwards*   54

To Autumn | *John Keats*   58

Puritan Reflections on Nature as a Revelation of God | *Thomas Shepherd, Thomas Taylor, and Richard Baxter*   62

How Nature Illuminates Godliness | *Selections from Psalms and Proverbs*   66

Lines Written in Early Spring | *William Wordsworth*   70

Virtue | *George Herbert*   73

Great Moments of Epiphany in Nature | *William Cullen Bryant, Sidney Lanier, Charles Dickens, and Alfred, Lord Tennyson*   76

Day Is Dying in the West | *Mary Lathbury*   80

How Nature Is Always Changing | *Ralph Waldo Emerson*   84

Lines Written in Kensington Gardens | *Matthew Arnold*   88

Walking in Nature | *Selections from the Song of Solomon and Jonathan Edwards*   92

Birds, ca. 1840

To Daffodils | *Robert Herrick* 96

How God Blesses Us through Nature | *Nathaniel Hawthorne* 99

I Sing the Mighty Power of God | *Isaac Watts* 102

Tintern Abbey | *William Wordsworth* 104

The Snow Storm | *Ralph Waldo Emerson* 108

The Voice from the Whirlwind | *Selections from Job 38* 110

The Archetypal River | *Medley* 114

Lessons from Nature | *Charles Spurgeon* 118

Communing with God through Nature | *George Washington Carver* 123

God's Grandeur | *Gerard Manley Hopkins* 127

These All Look to You | *Psalm 104* 130

The House That God Built and Furnished | *Martin Luther and Caedmon* 135

A Prayer in Spring | *Robert Frost* 140

Like a Bridegroom Leaving His Chamber | *King David and Mark Twain* 143

This Is My Father's World | *Maltbie D. Babcock* 147

Nature in Paradise | *John Milton* 150

The Beauty of the World | *Jonathan Edwards* 154

Let Them Praise the Name of the Lord | *Psalm 148* 158

Notes   163

Image Credits   169

Scripture Index   176

Dish with rocks, flowers, and birds (Japanese), 1710–30

Introduction

THE UNIFYING ELEMENT OF THIS ANTHOLOGY is its subject matter. All its selections and accompanying visuals take nature for their content. As the entries unfold, they have the effect of turning a prism in the light as they illuminate more and more facets of nature.

By giving us selections by diverse authors spanning many centuries and writing in numerous genres, this anthology presents a similar kaleidoscope of literary forms. Until recently, such a book would have also been called an anthology of nature writing, but that designation now denotes expository or informational writing about the natural environment. Most of this is propagandistic prose whose purpose is to advance the cause of earth keeping. By contrast, the entries in this anthology meet the three criteria that allow us to identify them as works of literature.

The literary author's first task is to present some aspect of human experience for our contemplation. Teachers of literature and writing commonly tell their students that literature *shows* rather than *tells*. To "show" is to present a subject so concretely that readers vicariously experience it in their imaginations. To "tell" is to explain a subject abstractly and as a set of ideas. Whereas expository prose tells us *about* a subject, a literary text *presents* the subject. None of the entries in this anthology develops a thesis about nature the way an informational essay would. The authors do, indeed, hope to persuade us of certain things regarding nature and prompt us to action, but their approach is literary rather than expository.

Part of this approach involves a specific technique that sets off literary writing about nature from literature as a whole. This distinctive feature is the author as a prominent presence in the text. For example, many nature poems begin by placing their speaker in a landscape—so many that there is a book on English Romanticism titled *Poets in the Landscape*. And even when the author or speaker is not situated in a scene of nature, we as readers *are* so situated by virtue of the author's descriptions.

Introduction

Nature authors are not content simply to assert the truth about nature; they also make themselves, and therefore us, participants in an implied action. As we read the entries in this anthology, we repeatedly feel as though we are accompanying their authors on an excursion into nature. This is partly explicable by the authors' literary impulse to render a subject so concretely that we vicariously experience in our imaginations the events they are describing. By helping us to experience nature, the authors gain credibility regarding their assertions about nature. We intuitively understand that the content of each passage grows out of the experience of an actual person. The literature of nature, be it poetry or prose, uses the author as evidential proof.

The literary author's second task is to offer an interpretation of the experiences that he or she has placed before readers for contemplation. For this reason, texts that record a moment or scene in nature, and no more than that, have been omitted from this anthology. As delightful as such bits and pieces are, they are insubstantial. Great literature prompts us to think about a subject as well as to vicariously experience it. Further, because this anthology is devotional in intention, its entries either espouse a Christian view of nature or express a viewpoint that is consonant with Christianity and easily nudged in that direction by the commentary that accompanies the selections.

The literary author's third task is to imbue a text with artistic form and beauty for our enjoyment and aesthetic enrichment. All the entries in this anthology flaunt their writers' verbal artistry and literary craftsmanship. We might note in passing that of all the poems in the Old Testament book of Psalms, those on nature are among the most dense with poetic technique. It is easy to see why the literature of nature is characterized by pronounced artistry: nature itself is a work of art. It readily encourages authors to draw on their full literary resources and skill.

As we read the entries in this anthology, we are helped by taking a trip back in time to the contemplative exercises of the Middle Ages. These exercises began with "composing the scene": imagining oneself as present at an event in the Bible. One then subjected the scene to analysis with the goal of understanding it fully. Finally, one reached closure, usually either by turning to God in prayer or by codifying what today we call an action plan or statement of resolve to act.

This three-part paradigm is universal throughout poetry and poetic prose. Entry after entry of this anthology begins by placing its speaker, and therefore us as well, in a natural setting. Thus placed, we accompany the speaker in analyzing the meaning of what we observe or experience. The lyric texts display one of two tendencies: they are either reflective (meaning that they enact a thought process) or affective or emotional (meaning that they display a set of feelings). Each poem or prose passage then concludes with an explicit or implied action plan for us. The selections within this anthology often present these three elements of observation, analysis, and resolution in a fluid manner instead of a three-part sequence, but we can arrange our reading experience of all of them according to this paradigm.

Léon Richet, *The Spring*, 1882

Introduction

What does nature literature add to our lives? Four things. First, such literature often gives us new experiences of nature, taking us to places and showing us plants and landscapes that we ourselves have not encountered. We can therefore read this anthology as a travelogue to the unknown.

Yet many entries in this anthology give expression to experiences of nature that are familiar and beloved to us. In these cases, the author serves as our representative by expressing what we too have experienced, thought, and felt—and with the added bonus of expressing it better than we can. The authors give shape to our own treasured experiences of nature, reminding us of them and enabling us to celebrate them. By giving us a mental itinerary of scenes we plan to visit or suggesting adjustments we can make to our lifestyles, they help us to enhance our own contact with nature.

Third, even when experiences that we read about themselves are familiar, literature presents them in a new and striking way. For example, just as we experience a bowl of fruit on a table in a fresh way when we see it portrayed in a still life painting, literary authors likewise compel our attention and expand our insight into familiar experiences through their writing. When the psalmist depicts God as giving "snow like wool" and scattering "frost like ashes" (Ps. 147:16), we look at snow and frost in a different way.

Joris Hoefnagel, *A Tiger, a Lynx, and a Jaguar(?); A Pair of Bohemian Waxwings, a Shelduck(?), and a Brant Goose with a Ginger Plant*, ca. 1575/1580

Introduction

For Christians, a fourth gift we receive from immersing ourselves in literary depictions of nature is an informed and biblical view of nature. Of all the subjects that currently require a well-thought-out and defensible Christian viewpoint, nature surely ranks in the top tier. It is often neglected among Christians and from the pulpit. We cannot afford to be ignorant about such an important subject, and this anthology will help to broaden our understanding.

The overall goal of this anthology is to enable nature to be all that it can be in our lives. God created nature to bless us. He does not wish us to neglect such a great gift. Under this overall goal, the individual entries and their accompanying explications serve a range of purposes. One is to celebrate certain features of nature. Another is to set our affections or emotions in right tune (to borrow John Milton's delightful phrase). A note of exhortation is also prominent—one that encourages us to do better. A plausible order of festivities is first to read an entry, then to study its commentary and devotional note, and finally to reread the text in light of any new understanding gained.

Nature literature, as already hinted, tends to be *super* literature. The artistry of nature has a way of bringing out the best from authors who write about it. The visuals that accompany the verbal fireworks in this anthology offer the proverbial "two for the price of one." ▪

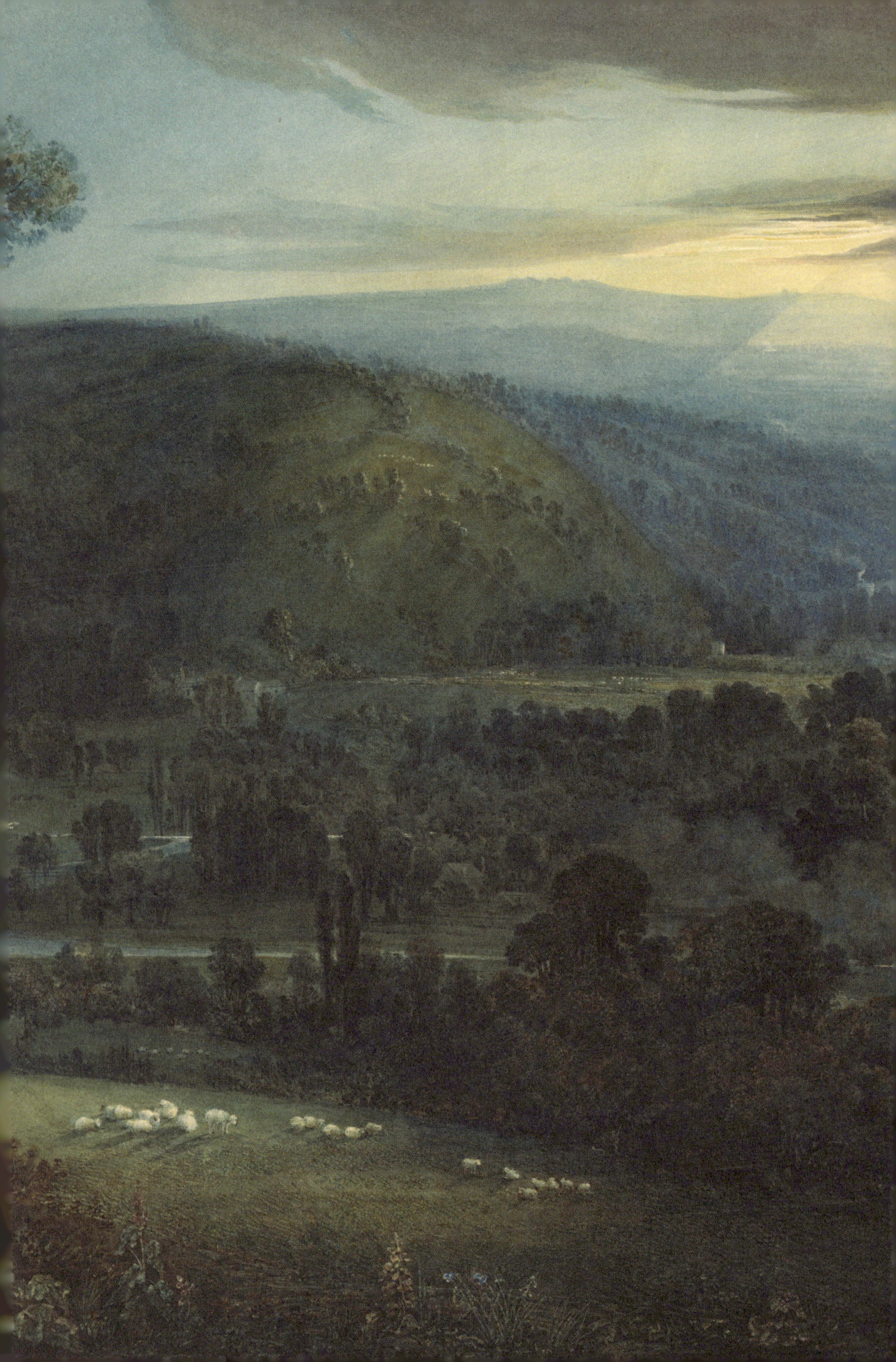

God Visits the Earth

Psalm 65:5–13

By awesome deeds you answer us with righteousness,
    O God of our salvation,
the hope of all the ends of the earth
    and of the farthest seas;

the one who by his strength established the mountains,
    being girded with might;
who stills the roaring of the seas,
    the roaring of their waves,
    the tumult of the peoples,
so that those who dwell at the ends of the earth
    are in awe at your signs.

You make the going out of the morning and the evening
    to shout for joy.
You visit the earth and water it;
    you greatly enrich it;
the river of God is full of water;
    you provide their grain,
    for so you have prepared it.
You water its furrows abundantly,
    settling its ridges,
softening it with showers,
    and blessing its growth.

You crown the year with your bounty;
    your wagon tracks overflow with abundance.
The pastures of the wilderness overflow,
    the hills gird themselves with joy,
the meadows clothe themselves with flocks,
    the valleys deck themselves with grain,
    they shout and sing together for joy. ∎

William Turner of Oxford, *Dawn in the Valley*, 1832

EXPRESSED AS A PRAYER TO GOD, this psalm has nearly everything we expect in a nature poem. Reinforcing the premise that nature is solidly theocentric, the controlling idea is asserted in the middle of the poem: *You visit the earth.* The poem presents nature as both the scene of God's visitation and the evidence of it.

The poem is organized into four units, which are printed above as stanzas. The first is an exalted four-line invocation to God. Even though its focus is on *our salvation* rather than on nature, it nonetheless introduces the latter with the imagery of *the earth* and *the farthest seas.*

As the poem shifts to focus on nature in its second stanza, it continues to evidence the spirit of the sublime that has dominated its invocation. We move in a world of *mountains* established by God's *strength* and *might*, of *roaring . . . seas*, and of people *at the ends of the earth* who are *in awe* at God's *signs*. God here visits the earth as a transcendent deity who controls the cosmos and reins in its *tumult.*

The main business of this nature poem comes to the fore as its third stanza shifts from the sublime to the picturesque. Pictures of gentle action in smaller spheres now dominate. In *Reflections on the Psalms*, C. S. Lewis observes that in Old Testament times, nearly everyone lived on the land, not in cities. Thus, for them, "what we call 'the country' is simply the world." The psalmists spend little time on landscape in their poetry, he claims, and instead "give us . . . the very feel of weather—weather . . . enjoyed almost as a vegetable might be supposed to enjoy it."

Who can doubt that this is true? In this third stanza, the poet gives us a close-up picture of rain falling on cropland. Anyone who has lived on a farm can resonate with the deep inner feeling of relief and gratitude when crops are watered and drought averted. A spirit of hope and anticipation prevails in this stanza, expressed especially in the phrases *you provide their grain* and *blessing its growth*. This is a summer stanza through and through.

The poem's fourth stanza moves to autumn harvest and fulfillment. It strikes its keynote within its opening line: *You crown the year with your bounty*. This stanza gains its effects with a common technique of nature poetry: namely, personification—treating inanimate features of nature as though they are people. Personification expresses a close kinship between people and nature. Here various features of nature are portrayed as people who are dressing for a celebration.

The strength of this poem's metaphor—nature is a visit from God—makes it the ideal portal through which to enter this anthology. In a sense, all the selections in this anthology are variations on this theme. God created nature, and he sustains it moment by moment. We ourselves can profitably think about how our experience of nature might be rectified and enriched if we viewed it as our own visit from God. ■

For all its tone of celebration, Psalm 65 contains an implied exhortation as well. In Luke 19:44, Jesus warns about the judgment God will bring against people who "did not know the time of [their] visitation." Responding appropriately to nature is one way of preparing ourselves for the second coming of our God.

Jean-François Millet, *Haystacks: Autumn*, ca. 1874

God's Presence in Nature

Martin Luther (1483–1546)

The power of God ... is uncircumscribed and immeasurable, beyond and above all that is or may be. On the other hand, it must be essentially present at all places, even in the tiniest tree leaf. The reason is this: It is God who creates, effects, and preserves all things through his almighty power and right hand, as our Creed confesses. For he dispatches no officials or angels when he creates or preserves something, but all this is the work of his divine power itself. If he is to create or preserve it, however, he must be present and must make and preserve his creation both in its innermost and outermost aspects. Therefore, indeed, he himself must be present in every single creature in its innermost and outermost being, on all sides, through and through, below and above, before and behind, so that nothing can be more truly present and within all creatures than God himself with his power. ...

God has found the way whereby his own divine nature can be wholly and entirely in all creatures and in every single individual being, more deeply, more inwardly, more present than the creature is to itself, and yet on the other hand may and can be circumscribed nowhere and in no being, so that he actually embraces all things. . . . Then if his power and Spirit are present everywhere and in all things to the innermost and outermost degree, through and through, as it must be if he is to make and preserve all things everywhere, then his divine right hand, nature, and majesty must also be everywhere. He must surely be present if he makes and preserves them. . . .

God wants to be praised for nourishing and cherishing, for He cherishes all creatures. He is not only the Creator, but He is also the Sustainer and Nourisher.

God is wholly present in all creation, in every corner. He is behind you and before you. Do you think he is sleeping on a pillow in heaven? He is watching over you and protecting you.

What [glorious] thoughts people might have . . . about the fact that God is in all creatures, and so might reflect on the power and the wisdom of God in even the smallest flowers. Of a truth, who can imagine how God creates, out of the parched soil, such a variety of flowers, such beautiful colors, such sweet vernal grass, beyond anything that a painter . . . could make . . . ? If God can take such delight in our earthly sojourn, what must it be like in the life to come? ■

God's Presence in Nature

MARTIN LUTHER, A LEADER OF THE PROTESTANT REFORMATION, was so linked to the study and pulpit that his enthusiasm for nature may be surprising. Luther's response to seeing luxuriant fields of wheat is entirely typical of him: "O Lord, . . . all in and around thee are miracles. Thy voice causes to spring out of the earth, and out of the sand of the desert, these beautiful plants, these green blades, which so rejoice the eye."

This entry from Luther is one of the most important ones in this anthology, but in order to see why this is the case, we need to place his claims into the context of historical thought about God and nature. A key doctrine within Christian theology is that God is both transcendent (separate from the created order) and immanent (present within the natural

previous: Karl Gaff, *Canadian Pond Weed Leaf Tip*, 2021
this page: John La Farge, *Nocturne*, ca. 1885

order). The primary thrust of this passage is to assert God's immanence. The energy with which Luther makes this point may seem repetitious, but Luther's zeal in hammering the point home is entirely warranted. A single-minded focus on salvation history leads many to neglect and disparage nature. When we recognize this, we see that Luther's assertions can serve as a corrective to a narrow view of God and his work.

Yet it is also possible to overshoot the mark in regard to God's immanence. Ancient mythology deified nature, and so has the Romantic movement of the last two centuries. The heresy particular to Romanticism is called pantheism, which *equates* God, people, and nature. Such a view puts forth the objects of nature as themselves divine. A close reading of Luther's discussion in this passage shows how careful he is to show that (1) God is *present in* nature, but no more, and (2) God is *beyond and above all that is or may be*.

If one purpose of his passage is thus to correct error and heresy, another is doxological—devoted to praising God. The passage conveys this particularly through the synonyms that it heaps up—it describes God as present *in every single creature in its innermost and outermost being, on all sides, and through, below and above, before and behind*. Luther does not simply assert God's immanence; he is enraptured by it. We can also relish his characteristic touch of imaginative realism when he asserts that God is not *sleeping on a pillow in heaven*.

Our takeaway from this passage follows the same contour as our analysis: we can use it to lead us to think clearly about the doctrines of God's transcendence and immanence, to steer clear of the aberration of pantheism, and to render praise to God, who *wants to be praised for nourishing and cherishing . . . . all creatures*. ■

Like Luther, the Christ hymn in Colossians 1 asserts that Christ is both transcendent over nature and immanent in it: "By him all things were created, in heaven and on earth. . . . And he is before all things, and in him all things hold together" (vv. 16–17).

Bird on her nest (Japan), 1800s

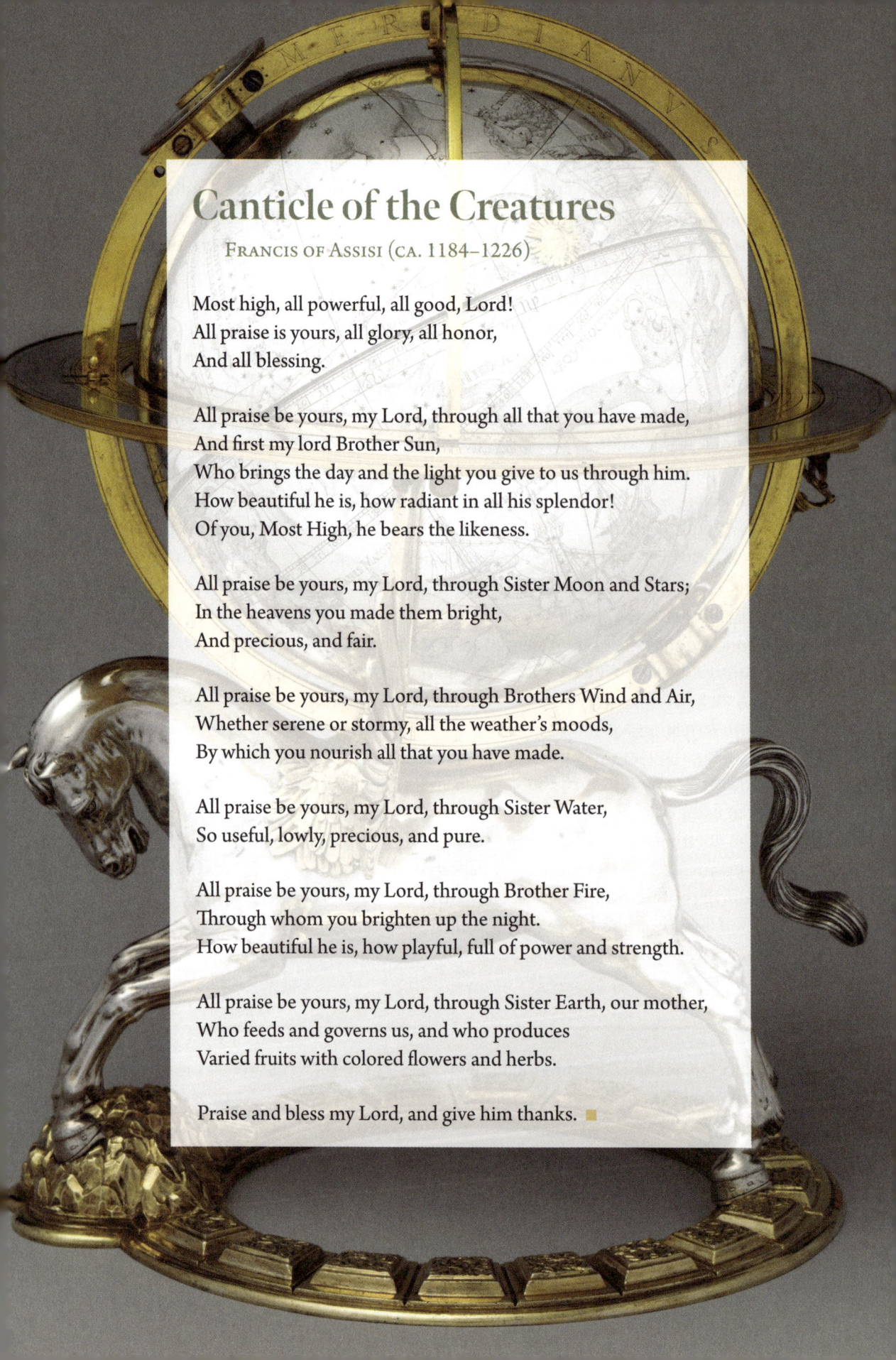

Canticle of the Creatures

Francis of Assisi (ca. 1184–1226)

Most high, all powerful, all good, Lord!
All praise is yours, all glory, all honor,
And all blessing.

All praise be yours, my Lord, through all that you have made,
And first my lord Brother Sun,
Who brings the day and the light you give to us through him.
How beautiful he is, how radiant in all his splendor!
Of you, Most High, he bears the likeness.

All praise be yours, my Lord, through Sister Moon and Stars;
In the heavens you made them bright,
And precious, and fair.

All praise be yours, my Lord, through Brothers Wind and Air,
Whether serene or stormy, all the weather's moods,
By which you nourish all that you have made.

All praise be yours, my Lord, through Sister Water,
So useful, lowly, precious, and pure.

All praise be yours, my Lord, through Brother Fire,
Through whom you brighten up the night.
How beautiful he is, how playful, full of power and strength.

All praise be yours, my Lord, through Sister Earth, our mother,
Who feeds and governs us, and who produces
Varied fruits with colored flowers and herbs.

Praise and bless my Lord, and give him thanks. ■

WE NEED TO START OUR ANALYSIS of this poem with a biographical fact: its author was a famous lover of nature. Francis of Assisi was an Italian monk of the early thirteenth century—the founder of the famous Franciscan order. His sense of kinship with animals became legendary in his own lifetime, and he is especially associated with birds. He called the creatures his brothers and sisters, and he exhorted them to praise God. All of this alerts us to the fact that his famous poem about creation was not just a poetic exercise but a codification of what the author practiced in his everyday life.

The first thing we notice about the poem is its simplicity. Its individual stanzas are brief, easily recognized units. Except for its enclosing first and last stanzas, each stanza follows the same format, beginning with an ascription of praise that is addressed to God as a prayer and repeated verbatim. The poem catalogs the familiar forces of nature in a manner that a child can easily follow, and to call the sun and moon brother and sister is something we might expect in a book for little children.

But there is actually a great deal of complexity at work below its simple surface, and our best entry into this depth is to dispel some common misconceptions and misrepresentations that surround the poem. First, the title most commonly attached to it, "Canticle of the Sun," is simply incorrect. Only one of its stanzas is about the sun; the rest of the poem is about other creatures of the cosmos. Second, the poem is not, as sometimes claimed, an imitation of Psalm 148. Like that psalm, it is a poem of praise that moves through the realms of nature from the sky to the earth. Psalm 148 is an extended doxology (a command to praise) that is addressed to created beings through a figure of speech known as apostrophe (an address delivered to something inanimate as though it were a person). By contrast, Francis of Assisi addresses his poem to God. Additionally, while this canticle shares *part* of the catalog of creation that Psalm 148 also presents, Francis is also working with a tradition built around the four elements: wind, water, fire, and earth.

The poem has the same overall effect that we find in the familiar psalms of praise—namely, one of exalting God for his work of creation. But as we look at the poem more closely, we see that this overall *effect* is the only thing it shares with those praise psalms. The psalms command fellow believers to praise God for creation, but Francis of Assisi does not command anyone. Instead he expresses a *wish* that God be praised—and

Gerhard Emmoser, Celestial globe with clockwork, 1579

not by people but by agents of nature. This wish for God be to praised also carries an implicit declaration that he is worthy of such praise. Even more surprising, Francis pictures God being praised not *for* creation but *through* it. This leads us to wonder what he means.

Three final aspects of the poem round out our admiration of it. The rhetorical technique of repetition is in full force both in its repetition of the line *All praise be yours, my Lord* and in its pattern of describing each creature that it names. Second, the poet's skill can be seen in the way he ascribes appropriate qualities to the various creatures that he names—light to the sun, for example, and fluctuating serenity and storminess to the wind. Finally, most striking of all is that familial imagery that he ascribes to the elements of nature by calling them *Brother* and *Sister*.

Our takeaway from this poem comes when we allow it to prompt us to analyze how God can be praised *through* or by means of creation as well as what implications result from viewing the elements of nature as our brothers and sisters.

"Canticle of the Creatures" expresses a prayer or wish for God to be praised through his creation. The Bible gives us pictures of that wish actually coming to pass. An example is Isaiah 55:12: "The mountains and the hills before you shall break forth into singing, and all the trees of the field shall clap their hands."

Jean-Baptiste-Camille Corot,
The Eel Gatherers, 1860/1865

For the Beauty of the Earth

Folliott S. Pierpoint (1835–1917)

For the beauty of the earth,
For the glory of the skies,
For the love which from our birth
Over and around us lies,
    Lord of all to thee we raise
    This our hymn of grateful praise.

For the beauty of each hour
Of the day and of the night,
Hill and vale and tree and flow'r,
Sun and moon and stars of light.
    Lord of all to thee we raise
    This our hymn of grateful praise.

For each perfect gift of thine
To our race so freely given,
Graces human and divine,
Flowers of earth, and buds of heaven:
    Lord of all to thee we raise
    This our hymn of grateful praise. ■

Joseph Mallord William Turner, *Keelmen Heaving in Coals by Moonlight*, 1835

FOLLIOTT PIERPOINT WAS A NATURE POET as well as a hymnwriter. "For the Beauty of the Earth" was inspired when the twenty-nine-year-old took a springtime walk on the hills surrounding his native city of Bath, England. Overwhelmed by the beauty of his surroundings, Pierpoint sat down in the midst of the landscape and composed a poem that, surprisingly, was first published as an eight-stanza Communion hymn. Eventually it became a familiar Thanksgiving hymn as later editors printed the stanzas that suited their purpose. Here we have selected three stanzas with the conventions of nature poetry in mind.

We will understand these conventions more readily if we take a brief excursion into the history of ideas about what constitutes nature. Starting at the beginning of the nineteenth century, a movement known as Romanticism conditioned people to think of nature as opposed to human civilization. Before that, people had viewed themselves as being part of nature. Psalm 148 provides a good illustration of this by placing people in the realm of nature alongside the hills and birds. In such a view, human emotions toward family and friends are natural and therefore part of "nature."

Pierpoint's poem expresses this older view in its opening stanza, which places before us three categories of nature: (1) the earth on which we live, (2) the sky above us, and (3) the human community of which we are a part. The second stanza then narrows its focus to non-human nature by picturing the panorama of the hourly and daily cycle, followed by a catalog of the elements that most readily enter our minds when the concept of nature is named: *hill, vale, tree, flower, sun, moon, stars*. The poet condenses what we often think of as nature poetry into just four lines.

In the third stanza, the poet moves from particular descriptions of nature to descriptions of all the things that we experience as part of God's creation. At first we might even think this stanza is leaving nature behind, but nature does remain on its agenda, albeit metaphorically. The blessings that the poem has been rehearsing throughout are called *flowers* here (representing the most beautiful things we know on earth) and *buds* (foreshadowings of heavenly glories to come).

With its short lines and simple *ababcc* rhyme scheme, the poem can be easily grasped. Yet its syntax, or sentence structure, introduces a pleasing element of complexity. This can be attributed to two things. First, the lines do not follow the ordinary order of clauses in which a subject is stated first and then followed by a predicate (the verb and other elements that complete the sentence's meaning). Instead, each stanza begins with a subordinate clause that is introduced by the preposition *for*. This format is combined with a suspended sentence structure, in which the verb that completes the meaning is withheld for a long time—four whole lines, in fact. Tension builds up and is finally released in the refrain, which completes the thought of each stanza.

We can apply this poem by allowing it, despite its brevity, to make us aware of how pervasive nature is in our daily lives. Once it has, we can enthusiastically allow the praise of the refrain to become our prayer to God. ■

This poem puts into practice what Psalm 105:2 commands: "Sing to [God], sing praises to him; tell of all his wondrous works!"

Richard Wilson, *Lake Albano*, 1762

It Is the First Mild Day of March

William Wordsworth (1770–1850)

It is the first mild day of March,
Each minute sweeter than before;
The redbreast sings from the tall larch
That stands beside our door.

There is a blessing in the air,
Which seems a sense of joy to yield
To the bare trees, and mountains bare,
And grass in the green field.

Love, now a universal birth,
From heart to heart is stealing,
From earth to man, from man to earth:
It is the hour of feeling.

One moment now may give us more
Than years of toiling reason:
Our minds shall drink at every pore
The spirit of the season.

Some silent laws our hearts will make,
Which they shall long obey:
We for the year to come may take
Our temper from today.

And from the blessed power that rolls
About, below, above,
We'll frame the measure of our souls:
They shall be tuned to love.

THE VERSION OF THE SEASONAL poem that appears here omits three stanzas from Wordsworth's original composition, in which the poet addresses his sister and invites her to spend a day with him soaking in all that springtime offers. These stanzas have not been included here because they detract from the universality of the poem, but one of their features still carries over—it remains a poem of invitation. We should read it as inviting us, and not simply Wordsworth's sister, to yield ourselves to nature.

The poem is organized according to a three-part contemplative paradigm that can be traced all the way back to the Middle Ages. Its first two stanzas compose the scene: they give us just enough description to activate our own memories of early springtime and engage our imaginations.

Once this appeal to our memory and imagination has set the scene, the poem's middle two stanzas subject the scene to analysis. Wordsworth emphasizes nature's ability to induce strong feelings in us. The moral and spiritual power of nature, and its healing effect on the human psyche, were Wordsworth's greatest poetic themes. In case we find ourselves resisting Wordsworth's exalted claims about nature, we should

Deepak Sundar, *European Robin Looks*, 2019

remember that he is extending an invitation for us to give what he says a try—to *yield* to nature and find its *blessing* (stanza 2). We cannot legitimately object before doing so.

The poem's concluding pair of stanzas gives us an action plan. The religious language that the poem has kept latent up to this point now becomes dominant. Thus we read about *our hearts* making *silent laws* that we *shall long obey*, about *the blessed power that rolls about, below, above*, and about *[framing] the measure of our souls*. The poet proposes an encounter with nature in such a way that Christian readers can align his words with their faith. No suspicion should attach to Wordsworth's religious language in the last stanza, where he clearly avoids the pantheistic claim that the divine power of nature resides in nature.

So far this analysis has viewed the poem as a seasonal composition, a religious nature poem, and a poem of invitation. Two additional labels will fill out our picture of it. The poem has the character of a manifesto—one in which Wordsworth outlines what he believes nature stands ready to give us. He emphasizes three things: personal joy and wellbeing, a rich emotional life, and the ability to live a life of love. Finally, this work can be called a poem of rapture, since the poet gives full vent to the feelings he experiences when surrounded by nature. His implied claim is that we can share this rapture.

This poem has a double application: we can give its poet a sympathetic hearing as he makes his case for giving ourselves to nature, and we can take the further step of accepting the poem's invitation to see what encountering nature can do for us. ∎

Wordsworth's invitation for us to open ourselves to the beneficial influences of nature finds the following parallel in Job 12:

> But ask the beasts, and they will teach you;
> > the birds of the heavens, and they will tell you;
> or the bushes of the earth, and they will teach you;
> > and the fish of the sea will declare to you. (vv. 7–8)

> In [God's] hand is the life of every living thing
> > and the breath of all mankind. (v. 10)

Rembrandt Peale, *Rubens Peale with a Geranium*, 1801

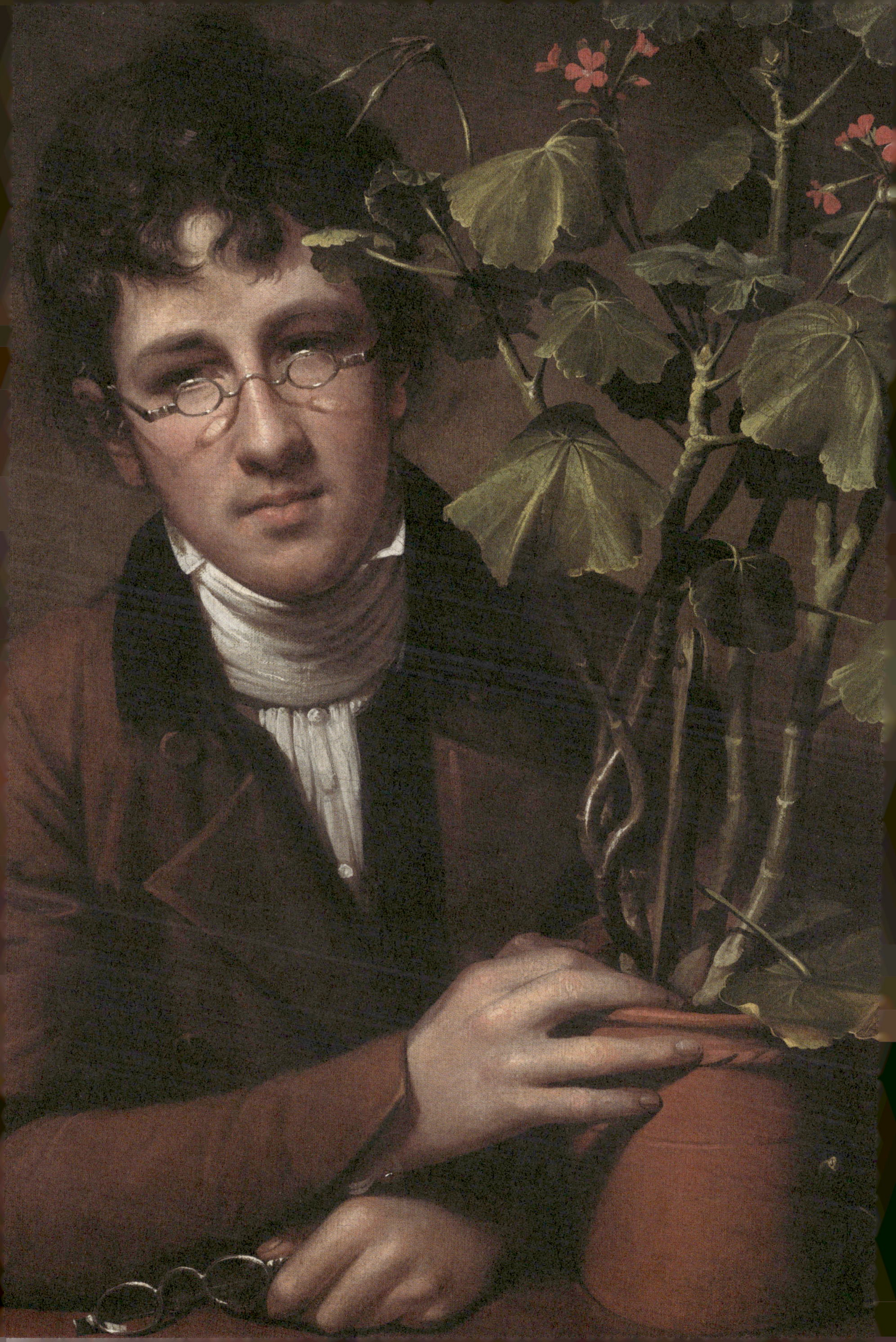

Prayers about Nature
Book of Common Prayer

Accept, O Lord, our thanks and praise
   for all your gifts
     so freely bestowed upon us.

We thank you for the splendor of the whole creation,
   for the beauty of this world,
   in earth and sky and sea,
   and for the wonder of life.
We give you thanks, most gracious God,
   for the richness of mountains, plains, and rivers;
   for the songs of birds and the loveliness of flowers.
We praise you for these good gifts,
   and pray that we may
   safeguard them for our posterity.

Grant that we may continue to grow
   in our grateful enjoyment
   of your abundant creation,
to the honor and glory of your Name,
   now and forever.

Almighty God, in giving us dominion
   over things on earth,
   you made us fellow workers in your creation.
Give us wisdom and reverence
   so to use the resources of nature,
   that no one may suffer from our abuse of them,
so that generations yet to come
   may continue to praise you
   for your bounty.
Make us, we pray, ever thankful
   for your loving providence,
and grant that we, remembering the account
   that we must one day give,
   may be faithful stewards of your good gifts.

Prayers about Nature

O gracious Father, who opens your hand
   and fills all things living with plenteousness,
bless the lands and waters,
   and multiply the harvests of the world;
   let your Spirit go forth,
   that it may renew the face of the earth;
show your lovingkindness,
   that our land may give her increase.
By your Son Jesus Christ you have promised
   to all those who seek your kingdom
   and its righteousness all things necessary
   to sustain their life.
Send us, we entreat you, rain and showers,
   that we may receive the fruits of the earth,
   to our comfort and to your honor,
   through Jesus Christ our Lord.

Most gracious God, by whose knowledge
   the depths are broken up
   and the clouds drop down the dew:
we yield thee hearty thanks and praise
   for the return of seed time and harvest,
   for the increase of the ground
   and the gathering in of its fruits,
   and for all other blessings of thy merciful providence
   bestowed upon us.

O heavenly Father,
   who has filled the world with beauty,
open our eyes to behold
   your gracious hand in all your works,
that, rejoicing in your whole creation,
   we may learn to serve you with gladness,
   for the sake of him
   through whom all things were made,
   your Son Jesus Christ our Lord. Amen.

Prayers about Nature

No ENTRY IN THIS ANTHOLOGY covers more aspects of nature than this mosaic from the prayer book, but we need to unpack its individual units with attentiveness in order to see this. A wide-angle view of the passage immediately shows that it encompasses the three main actors in the drama of nature. First, it is all addressed as a prayer to God, thus establishing him as its sovereign central character. At the same time, we are aware at every point that people—we and our fellow worshippers—are the ones expressing these prayers to God. And the subject of every unit of this selection is nature. God, people, and nature comprise the world of the passage, as they do our everyday lives. It is helpful to visualize these three agents as if they are points of a triangle, thereby demonstrating that each one is connected to the other two.

The main genre of the selection is prayer, and as it unfolds, it proves to include the three main modes of prayer: petition, thanksgiving, and praise. Once alerted to this agenda, we can easily recognize and enter into the spirit of each one as it appears. The three elements are subtly interwoven, so that, for example, we are led to petition God to be bountiful in providing for us through nature, and then to thank him for having been bountiful.

The view of nature on display in this selection corresponds to the one we find in the book of Psalms. Its early units focus on the aesthetic beauty of nature. The later units expand on how useful nature is to us as the means by which God provides what we need to sustain our lives. A unit on human stewardship of nature appears in the middle of the passage, which reminds us that both the beauty and the life-sustaining usefulness of nature are at stake in our conduct toward nature.

The passage will offer even more to us when we are receptive to the verbal beauty and craftsmanship that are the hallmark of the Book of Common Prayer. The lines of this entry flow smoothly and mellifluously. The language is elegant. The organization is likewise impeccable. Its opening unit introduces everything that follows: petition (through the word *accept*), thanks, and praise. The umbrella concept of the passage is that the various elements of nature are God's *gifts*. The last unit of the selection forms a summary and climax of the entire set of prayers by reminding us that nature has been their focus and then challenging us to channel its blessings into a life of service and worship to God.

As we read and ponder this collection of prayers, we apply it to our lives as we consider everything it says about how we should view nature and relate to God in light of it. ■

The foundation on which these individual prayers of thanks, praise, and petition rest is that God created nature and sustains his creatures by means of it and that it is therefore part of our spiritual life as well as our physical life. First Timothy 4:4–5 asserts this same truth:

> For everything created by God is good, and nothing is to be rejected if it is received with thanksgiving, for it is made holy by the word of God and prayer.

Camille Corot, *The Ferryman*, ca. 1865

The Theater of God's Glory

John Calvin (1509–1564)

The world ... is a theater erected for displaying the glory of God.... Let us not disdain to receive a pious delight from the works of God, which everywhere present themselves to view in this very beautiful theater of the world.... Everyone should seriously apply himself to a consideration of the works of God, being placed in this very splendid theater to be a spectator of them....

If we consider for what end God has created the various kinds of food, we shall find that he intended to provide not only for our necessity, but likewise for our pleasure and delight. So in clothing, he has had in view not mere necessity, but propriety and decency. In herbs, trees, and fruits, beside their various uses, his design has been to gratify us by graceful forms and pleasant odors.... And even the natural properties of things sufficiently indicate for what end, and to what extent, it is lawful to use them. But shall the Lord have endued flowers with such beauty, to present itself to our eyes, with such sweetness of smell, to impress our sense of smelling; and shall it be unlawful for our eyes to be affected with the beautiful sight, or our olfactory nerves with the agreeable odor? What! has he not made such a distinction of colors as to render some more agreeable than others? Has he not given to gold and silver, to ivory and marble, a beauty which makes them more precious than other metals or stones? In a word, has he not made many things worthy of our estimation, independently of any necessary use? . . .

For this . . . is, in the order of nature, the first lesson of faith, to remember that, whithersoever we turn our eyes, all the things which we behold are the works of God; and at the same time to consider, with pious meditation, for what end God created them. . . . God has wonderfully adorned heaven and earth with the utmost possible abundance, variety, and beauty, like a large and splendid mansion, most exquisitely and copiously furnished. . . . It is undoubtedly the will of the Lord, that we should be continually employed in this holy meditation; that, while we contemplate in all the creatures, as in so many mirrors, the infinite riches of his wisdom, justice, goodness, and power, we might not only take a transient and cursory view of them, but might long dwell on the idea, seriously and faithfully revolve it in our minds, and frequently recall it to our memory. ■

Severin Roesen, *Still Life: Flowers and Fruit*, 1850–55

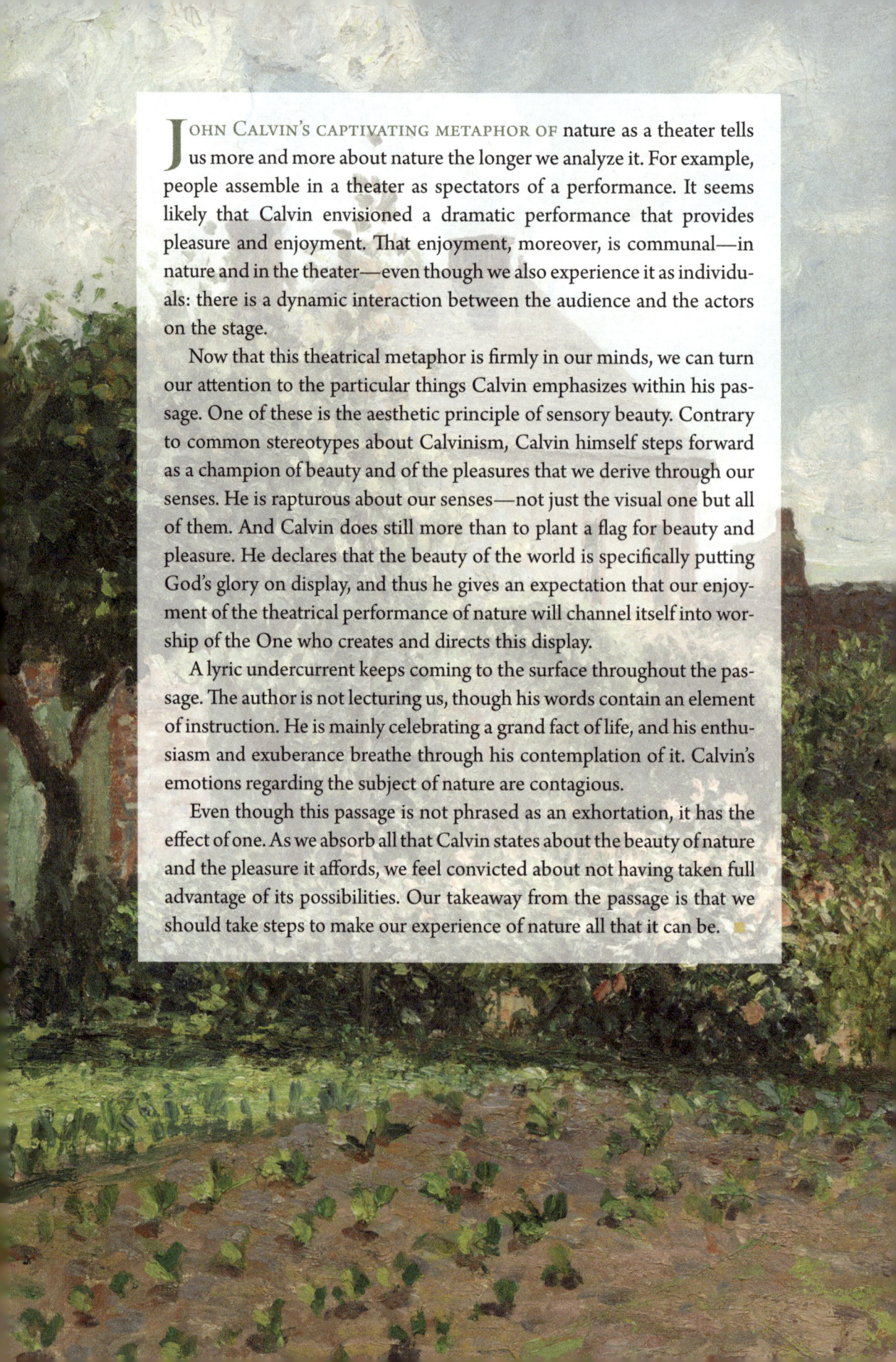

John Calvin's captivating metaphor of nature as a theater tells us more and more about nature the longer we analyze it. For example, people assemble in a theater as spectators of a performance. It seems likely that Calvin envisioned a dramatic performance that provides pleasure and enjoyment. That enjoyment, moreover, is communal—in nature and in the theater—even though we also experience it as individuals: there is a dynamic interaction between the audience and the actors on the stage.

Now that this theatrical metaphor is firmly in our minds, we can turn our attention to the particular things Calvin emphasizes within his passage. One of these is the aesthetic principle of sensory beauty. Contrary to common stereotypes about Calvinism, Calvin himself steps forward as a champion of beauty and of the pleasures that we derive through our senses. He is rapturous about our senses—not just the visual one but all of them. And Calvin does still more than to plant a flag for beauty and pleasure. He declares that the beauty of the world is specifically putting God's glory on display, and thus he gives an expectation that our enjoyment of the theatrical performance of nature will channel itself into worship of the One who creates and directs this display.

A lyric undercurrent keeps coming to the surface throughout the passage. The author is not lecturing us, though his words contain an element of instruction. He is mainly celebrating a grand fact of life, and his enthusiasm and exuberance breathe through his contemplation of it. Calvin's emotions regarding the subject of nature are contagious.

Even though this passage is not phrased as an exhortation, it has the effect of one. As we absorb all that Calvin states about the beauty of nature and the pleasure it affords, we feel convicted about not having taken full advantage of its possibilities. Our takeaway from the passage is that we should take steps to make our experience of nature all that it can be.

Psalm 19:1–2 corroborates Calvin's claim that nature is a continuous display of divine glory, of which we are spectators:

> The heavens declare the glory of God,
>   and the sky above proclaims his handiwork.
> Day to day pours out speech,
>   and night to night reveals knowledge.

Famous Hymns Inspired by Nature

AUGUSTUS TOPLADY (1740–1778),
HENRY VAN DYKE (1852–1933),
AND ANNIE HAWKS (1936–1918)

"Rock of Ages"

Rock of Ages, cleft for me
Let me hide myself in thee;
Let the water and the blood,
From thy riven side which flowed,
Be of sin the double cure,
Cleanse me from its guilt and power.

"Joyful, Joyful, We Adore Thee"

Joyful, joyful, we adore Thee,
God of glory, Lord of love;
Hearts unfold like flowers before Thee,
Opening to the sun above.
Melt the clouds of sin and sadness;
Drive the dark of doubt away;
Giver of immortal gladness,
Fill us with the light of day!

All Thy works with joy surround Thee,
Earth and heaven reflect Thy rays,
Stars and angels sing around Thee,
Center of unbroken praise.
Field and forest, vale and mountain,
Flowery meadow, flashing sea,
Singing bird and flowing fountain
Call us to rejoice in Thee.

"I Need Thee Every Hour"

I need Thee every hour,
Most gracious Lord;
No tender voice like Thine
Can peace afford. ■

Famous Hymns Inspired by Nature

NONE OF THE HYMNS IN THIS ENTRY is a nature hymn, though each contains a stanza or a pair of stanzas that focus on nature. The main purpose of this entry is to show that in some cases, a familiar hymn dealing with the spiritual life arose from an encounter, on a specific occasion, between its poet and nature. This itself can prompt us to think about how nature might influence our own walk with God.

According to the received lore surrounding "Rock of Ages," Augustus Toplady, a young cleric at the time, was walking along a road near his village when a thunderstorm struck. He took cover in a cave on the side of a rocky hill that had a vertical split or cleft in it. The words of a hymn based on this experience took root in the author's mind at that moment. Although the resulting work is not *about* the place and storm that occasioned it, it makes this refuge provided by a cave into a continuous metaphor for Christ's sacrifice on the cross and the shelter it provides from God's judgment against sin.

"Joyful, Joyful, We Adore Thee" is a hymn of praise. Henry Van Dyke titled his poem "Hymn of Joy" and wrote it so that it could be set to the music of Beethoven's "Ode to Joy," from the final movement of his Ninth Symphony. The author claimed that the poem was inspired by the Berkshire mountains in Massachusetts, which he was visiting as a guest speaker at the time he composed it. According to his son, Van Dyke's intention was to celebrate "a joy to be found in nature by the [person] who finds his first joy in living his own life in Jesus Christ." This intention fits the finished hymn exactly—two of its stanzas are nature poetry, and two of them celebrate the love of God.

Without knowing the details behind the composition of "I Need Thee Every Hour," we would never guess that it was inspired by nature—and, additionally, that it grew out of great joy rather than adversity. Here is author Annie Hawks's own account: "I remember well the morning, many years ago, when in the midst of the daily cares of my home, then in a distant city, I was so filled with the sense of nearness to the Master that, wondering how one could live without Him, either in joy or pain, these words were ushered into my mind, the thought at once taking full possession of me.... Seating myself by the open window in the balmy air of the bright June day, I caught my pencil and the words were soon committed to paper."

To apply what has been said in this entry, we need to let the point register that these hymnic poems, which were inspired by encounters with

previous: Camille Pissarro, *The Artist's Garden at Eragny*, 1898;
John Brett, *Kynance*, 1888

nature, go on to ultimately cover many aspects of the spiritual life. Then we can consider how our own souls might be similarly nurtured by our spending time in nature and allowing its effects to permeate us. ▪

Behind each of these three hymnic poems is a striking experience of nature that brought their authors into an understanding of God and the spiritual life. The same thing happens near the end of the book of Job, when the protagonist is brought into a deeper relation with God as he is led to ponder the wonders of nature. In response to this nature lesson, Job tells God, "I had heard of you by the hearing of the ear, but now my eye sees you" (Job 42:5).

Joseph Rodefer DeCamp,
The Seamstress, 1916

The Sun Also Rises, and the Sun Goes Down

WILLIAM WORDSWORTH (1770–1850)

"Earth Has Not Anything to Show More Fair"

Earth has not anything to show more fair:
Dull would he be of soul who could pass by
A sight so touching in its majesty.
This City now doth, like a garment, wear
The beauty of the morning; silent, bare,
Ships, towers, domes, theaters, and temples lie
Open unto the fields, and to the sky,
All bright and glittering in the smokeless air.
Never did sun more beautifully steep
In his first splendor valley, rock, or hill;
Ne'er saw I, never felt, a calm so deep!
The river glideth at his own sweet will.
Dear God! the very houses seem asleep;
And all that mighty heart is lying still!

"It Is a Beauteous Evening, Calm and Free"

It is a beauteous evening, calm and free;
The holy time is quiet as a nun
Breathless with adoration; the broad sun
Is sinking down in its tranquility;
The gentleness of heaven is on the sea.
Listen! the mighty Being is awake,
And doth with his eternal motion make
A sound like thunder—everlastingly.

The Sun Also Rises, and the Sun Goes Down

THE MOST RECURRENT CYCLE WE ENCOUNTER within nature is the daily one demarcated by sunrises and sunsets. A famous lyric titled "Sunrise, Sunset," from the musical *Fiddler on the Roof*, highlights how a succession of sunrises and sunsets gradually constitutes a person's life. Wordsworth's poetic descriptions of how days begin and end focus instead on the beauty of a specific sunrise and a specific sunset, prompting us to revel in the present moment as we share it with the poet.

Although Wordsworth did not compose these two poems to be companions, they fit together perfectly. They are occasional poems, meaning they arise from a specific occasion in the author's life. In 1802, Wordsworth made a journey from England to France. His coach left London in the early morning, heading for the seaport of Dover and the English Channel. The first poem in this entry records what he saw and felt as he crossed Westminster Bridge near the Houses of Parliament. A few days later, as he was walking on the French beach at sunset, Wordsworth experienced something equally spectacular and numinous.

Both poems combine a description of a scene with a record of the speaker's emotional response to it, thereby meeting the criterion of the major nineteenth-century Romantic genre known as a meditative landscape poem. The poems are written in such an emotional way that Wordsworth presents the visual aspects of both scenes as being filtered through his consciousness. The main feeling they are thus conveying is not excitement but calm. Regarding the sunrise, the poet claims that he has *never felt a calm so deep*. The second poem describes the sun as *sinking down in its tranquility* and leading *the gentleness of heaven* to brood over the sea. This is mood poetry at its best.

In addition to sharing all these things at the content level, the language of both is archaic and elegant—and for a very good reason. Wordsworth was following the model of the King James Bible, which was the leading influence on English and American literature from the sixteenth century through the twentieth. Its style fits perfectly with the religious quality that is subtly present in both these poems. For example, the churches seen from Westminster Bridge are called *temples*. The morning scene is said to be as beautiful as the first morning in Paradise. Unable to contain himself, the poet finally blurts out an address to God. Then, in order to capture the spirit of the *holy time* he experienced during the evening of the following poem, Wordsworth chooses a religious simile to compare it to *a nun breathless with adoration*. He also goes on to claim that the presence of God—*the mighty Being*—is in the scene.

In addition to prompting us to treasure the sunrise and sunset when we have the opportunity to experience them, these poems encourage us to relate to God and to nature by means of our feelings. ▪

Wordworth's poems confirm the psalmist's declaration to God that "those who dwell at the ends of the earth are in awe at your signs. You make the going out of the morning and the evening to shout for joy" (Ps. 65:8).

Worthington Whittredge, *Second Beach, Newport*, 1865

Jesus' Command to Imitate Nature

Matthew 6:25–34

Therefore I tell you,
do not be anxious about your life,
    what you will eat
    or what you will drink,
nor about your body,
    what you will put on.
Is not life more than food,
    and the body more than clothing?

Look at the birds of the air:
    they neither sow nor reap
    nor gather into barns,
and yet your heavenly Father feeds them.

Are you not of more value than they?

And which of you by being anxious
    can add a single hour to his span of life?
And why are you anxious about clothing?
Consider the lilies of the field,
    how they grow:
they neither toil nor spin,
    yet I tell you, even Solomon in all his glory
    was not arrayed like one of these.

Jesus' Command to Imitate Nature

But if God so clothes the grass of the field,
   which today is alive
   and tomorrow is thrown into the oven,
will he not much more clothe you,
   O you of little faith?

Therefore do not be anxious, saying,
   "What shall we eat?"
   or "What shall we drink?"
   or "What shall we wear?"
For the Gentiles seek after all these things,
   and your heavenly Father knows that you need them all.
But seek first the kingdom of God
   and his righteousness,
   and all these things will be added to you.
Therefore do not be anxious about tomorrow,
   for tomorrow will be anxious for itself.
Sufficient for the day is its own trouble.

Jesus' Command to Imitate Nature

This passage is familiarly known as Jesus' discourse against anxiety. Several aspects of it, however, also invite us to analyze it as nature writing. The most important is that Jesus supports his argument that we should live free from worry by saying, in effect, "Take a look at the nature around you."

Before we unpack this appeal he makes to nature, we should absorb the masterful rhetoric of Jesus' discourse, which extends to both its organization and its style. The structure of the passage unfolds as follows: its opening unit states the thesis (*do not be anxious*) and applies it to the two spheres of *food* and *clothing*. If this opening is not quite within the realm of nature yet, it is not far from it, because the appeal it makes involves the way we maintain our earthly, physical lives.

Throughout the middle of the discourse, Jesus commands us to look at and consider three creatures of nature: *the birds, the lilies,* and *the grass of the field*. These are analogies as well as examples—analogies because Jesus is claiming that God's care for such creatures is like his care for us, and examples because he is commanding us to learn from them and imitate them. The long final section may not speak directly about nature, but it takes the lessons that Jesus expects us to learn from nature and applies them in a spiritual sense.

Three features of the style of this passage heighten its argument. One is the parallelism of its phrases and clauses, which produces a beauty that arrests our attention and inclines us to accept its message. The second is its repetition of key words and phrases, such as *eat* and *drink* and *clothe*—a repetition that drives the main point home. Most striking of all are its interspersed rhetorical questions, which Jesus asks not to elicit information but to move us to emotionally and intellectually assent to his commands.

The ways in which the passage proves to exemplify nature writing keep multiplying as we analyze it. First, its pictures of the birds, lilies, and grass are so memorable that they have been etched permanently in our minds and ensconced in our storehouse of sayings. Birds, lilies, and grass have never had greater immortality conferred upon them than through these lines. Second, Jesus leads us to view nature in a new light as he pictures birds, lilies, and grass as being like people who are fed and clothed. But this analogy works both ways: if they are like us, we too are like them by virtue of being objects of God's provision. In fact, this is the main argument of the discourse and its main takeaway for us: if creatures live free from anxiety because God provides for them, we need to shoulder *our* responsibility to trust God as fellow creatures. ◼

Elsewhere, too, Jesus appeals to nature in an argument that we should trust God to provide. An example is Luke 12:6–7: "Are not five sparrows sold for two pennies? And not one of them is forgotten before God. . . . Fear not; you are of more value than many sparrows."

previous: Coat (probably French), 1775–85
Joseph Bartholomew Kidd, *Sharp-Tailed Finch*, 1831/1833

The Rhodora
Ralph Waldo Emerson (1803–1882)

In May, when sea-winds pierced our solitudes,
I found the fresh rhodora in the woods,
Spreading its leafless blooms in a damp nook,
To please the desert and the sluggish brook.
The purple petals fallen in the pool
Made the black water with their beauty gay;
Here might the red-bird come his plumes to cool,
And court the flower that cheapens his array.
Rhodora, if the sages ask thee why
This charm is wasted on the earth and sky,
Tell them, dear, that if eyes were made for seeing,
Then beauty is its own excuse for being.
Why thou wert there, O rival of the rose,
I never thought to ask; I never knew,
But in my simple ignorance suppose
The self-same power that brought me there, brought you.

The Rhodora

THIS POEM BELONGS TO A GENRE known as the walking poem (also called the literature of the peripatetic) and to a subgenre known as the poem of discovery. In May of 1834, Ralph Waldo Emerson visited his extended family in New England. Going for a walk, he experienced what we read in this poem. The rhodora is a flowering shrub common in the swampy areas of New England. Its specific features, however, are unimportant to our experience with this poem; the flower that Emerson celebrates represents any beautiful flower we know that grows in obscurity and is therefore overlooked.

    The poem unfolds as most Romantic nature poems do. Emerson uses two separate phases to compose the scene, giving us four lines that narrate the moment he discovers the rhodora, followed by four lines that describe the experience more closely. Next, Emerson addresses the rhodora

17

directly, as though it were a person—a figure of speech called apostrophe. He is so enraptured by his newly found love that he even calls it *dear*.

Commentary on this poem regularly finds spiritual meanings beyond what the poem strictly dictates, alerting us to the presence of a subliminal level of Christian truth. At least four religious interpretations can be made. The first is the Christian virtue of humility, and an elevation of the common to a status of significance, along the lines of the claim made by 1 Corinthians 1:26–28 that God chooses the weak rather than the mighty. Second, and an extension of the first, is a rebuke for our tendency to ignore the beauty of nature in its hidden and humble forms. According to the poem, we are guilty if we do not pay attention to the small creatures in God's world.

Third, the poem stakes a very strong claim for the importance of beauty through its famous aphorism that *beauty is its own excuse for being*. Beauty does not require a utilitarian defense; it is enough that God created it and gave it as a gift to the human race. Finally, the poem's last line underscores the fact that people and nature are fellow dependents in God's creation.

On the technical side, the poem is divided into two halves. The first narrates and describes the poet's encounter with nature; the second is meditative. Each half of the poem begins with two rhyming couplets (consecutive lines that rhyme *aa, bb*) and is followed by a quatrain (rhyming *abab*).

The poet's journey of discovery and instructive session with us should lead us to be alert to hidden beauty in nature, value it and claim kinship with it, and acknowledge God as the maker of both nature and us.

As the foregoing analysis shows, it is amazing how much Emerson managed to encompass in a mere sixteen lines. Despite the multiplicity of ideas, the primary thrust is to plant a flag for beauty. Matching the splendor of Emerson's aphorism that "beauty is its own excuse for being" is the claim in Ecclesiastes 3:11 that God "has made everything beautiful in its time."

previous: Nikodem Nijaki, *Rhododendron smirnowii - blossom*, 2011
this page: Mark Catesby, *Rhododendron*, 1731–1754

Where Shall Beauty Be Found?

Edgar Allan Poe (1809–1849) and
Jonathan Edwards (1703–1758)

"The Poetic Principle" 1850

[We can find beauty] in the bright orbs that shine in Heaven . . . in the clustering of low shrubberies . . . in the waving of the grain-fields . . . in the slanting of tall eastern trees . . . in the blue distance of mountains . . . in the grouping of clouds . . . in the twinkling of half-hidden brooks . . . in the gleaming of silver rivers . . . in the repose of sequestered lakes . . . in the star-mirroring depths of lonely wells . . . in the songs of birds . . . in the sighing of the night-wind . . . in the repining voice of the forest . . . in the surf that complains to the shore . . . in the fresh breath of the woods . . . in the scent of the violet . . . in the voluptuous perfume of the hyacinth . . . [in the] oceans, illimitable and unexplored.

The Beauties of Nature, 1700s

THE SON OF GOD created the world for this very end, to communicate Himself in an image of His own excellency.... The beauties of nature are really emanations, or shadows, of the excellencies of the Son of God. So that when we are delighted with flowery meadows and gentle breezes of wind, we may consider that we only see the emanations of the sweet benevolence of Jesus Christ. When we behold the fragrant rose and lily, we see His love and purity. So the green trees and fields, and singing of birds, are the emanations of His infinite joy and benignity. The easiness and naturalness of trees and vines are shadows of His infinite beauty and loveliness. The crystal rivers and murmuring streams have the footsteps of His sweet grace and bounty.

When we behold the light and brightness of the sun, the golden edges of an evening cloud, or the beauteous bow, we behold the adumbrations of His glory and goodness and in the blue skies, we see His mildness and gentleness. There are also many things wherein we may behold His awful majesty: in the sun in its strength, in comets, in thunder, in the towering thunderclouds, in ragged rocks and the brows of mountains. That beauteous light with which the world is filled in a clear day is a lively shadow of His spotless holiness and happiness and delight in communicating Himself....

As God is infinitely the greatest Being, so he is allowed to be infinitely the most beautiful and excellent: and all the beauty to be found throughout the whole creation, is but the reflection of the diffused beams of that Being who has an infinite fullness of brightness and glory. ∎

Where Shall Beauty Be Found?

THE TITLE FOR THIS ENTRY is an allusion to the riveting question posed by Job 28 in the middle of its famous ode to wisdom. After celebrating the ingenuity that has allowed humans to discover the hidden wonders of nature, Job suddenly blurts out, "But where shall wisdom be found?" Similarly, the two authors for this entry focus our attention on where beauty can be found: in nature. This idea should seize our minds and emotions as we assimilate this entry.

Edgar Allan Poe led a tragic life filled with an endless succession of losses and abandonments. Yet there is much beauty and truth in the literature that he wrote, and his descendant Professor Harry Poe of Union

University wrote a book in which he raises the possibility (though not the certainty) that Poe was converted shortly before his death. Poe's beautiful paragraph within this entry, which exemplifies what literary scholars call prose poetry, is from an essay that describes the origin of poetry. In this famous essay, Poe defines a poem as the creation of beauty and then asks and answers the logical question of where such beauty can be found.

When we analyze the passage as nature writing, we see how Poe gives form and expression to our own cherished experiences of natural beauty. Poe does this very economically by means of the rhetorical technique known as the list or catalog. As he lists beautiful sights and sounds from nature, it is as though we are turning the pages of a book of nature photography or a scrapbook of photographs from family vacations. The passage awakens our memories and love of nature.

Jonathan Edwards fully supports Poe's endorsement of the beauty of nature. In fact, his imagination gravitates to the same images that Poe gives us—images such as *flowery meadows and gentle breezes, fragrant rose and lily, singing of birds, trees,* and *murmuring streams.* However, Edwards adds a level of beauty. He characteristically expresses a view, here and elsewhere in his writings, that the beauty of nature is an emanation of the supreme beauty of Christ and, by extension, of the triune God and the whole world of supernatural reality. Within such a framework, it is our responsibility to see more (though not less) in nature than simply its external forms.

Poe and Edwards step forward as expert guides for us to follow. Their writing overflows with images that awaken our own sense of the beauty of nature and prompt us to seek that beauty. And Edwards not only *asserts* the principle that the beauty of Christ can be found in nature but also gives *examples* of how this can be done, enabling us to put such an exercise into practice. ∎

The word *beauty* occurs over a hundred times in English translations of the Bible—and always in an overwhelmingly positive way. The passages by Poe and Edwards encourage us to allow the beauty of God to rest on us through the agency of nature; Psalm 90:17 expresses the same sentiment as a prayer: "Let the beauty of the Lord our God be upon us."

Wilhelm Amberg, *Young Woman Seated by a Stream (Contemplation),* before 1886

To Autumn

John Keats (1795–1821)

Season of mists and mellow fruitfulness,
Close bosom-friend of the maturing sun,
Conspiring with him how to load and bless
With fruit the vines that round the thatch-eaves run;
To bend with apples the mossed cottage-trees,
And fill all fruit with ripeness to the core;
To swell the gourd, and plump the hazel shells
With a sweet kernel; to set budding more,
And still more, later flowers for the bees,
Until they think warm days will never cease,
For Summer has o'er-brimmed their clammy cells.

Who hath not seen thee oft amid thy store?
Sometimes whoever seeks abroad may find
Thee sitting careless on a granary floor,
Thy hair soft-lifted by the winnowing wind;
Or on a half-reaped furrow sound asleep,
Drowsed with the fume of poppies, while thy hook
Spares the next swath and all its twinéd flowers:
And sometimes like a gleaner thou dost keep
Steady thy laden head across a brook;
Or by a cyder-press, with patient look,
Thou watchest the last oozings hours by hours.

Where are the songs of Spring? Ay, where are they?
Think not of them, thou hast thy music too,
While barred clouds bloom the soft-dying day,
And touch the stubble-plains with rosy hue;
Then in a wailful choir the small gnats mourn
Among the river sallows, borne aloft
Or sinking as the light wind lives or dies;
And full-grown lambs loud bleat from hilly bourn;
Hedge-crickets sing; and now with treble soft
The red-breast whistles from a garden-croft,
And gathering swallows twitter in the skies.

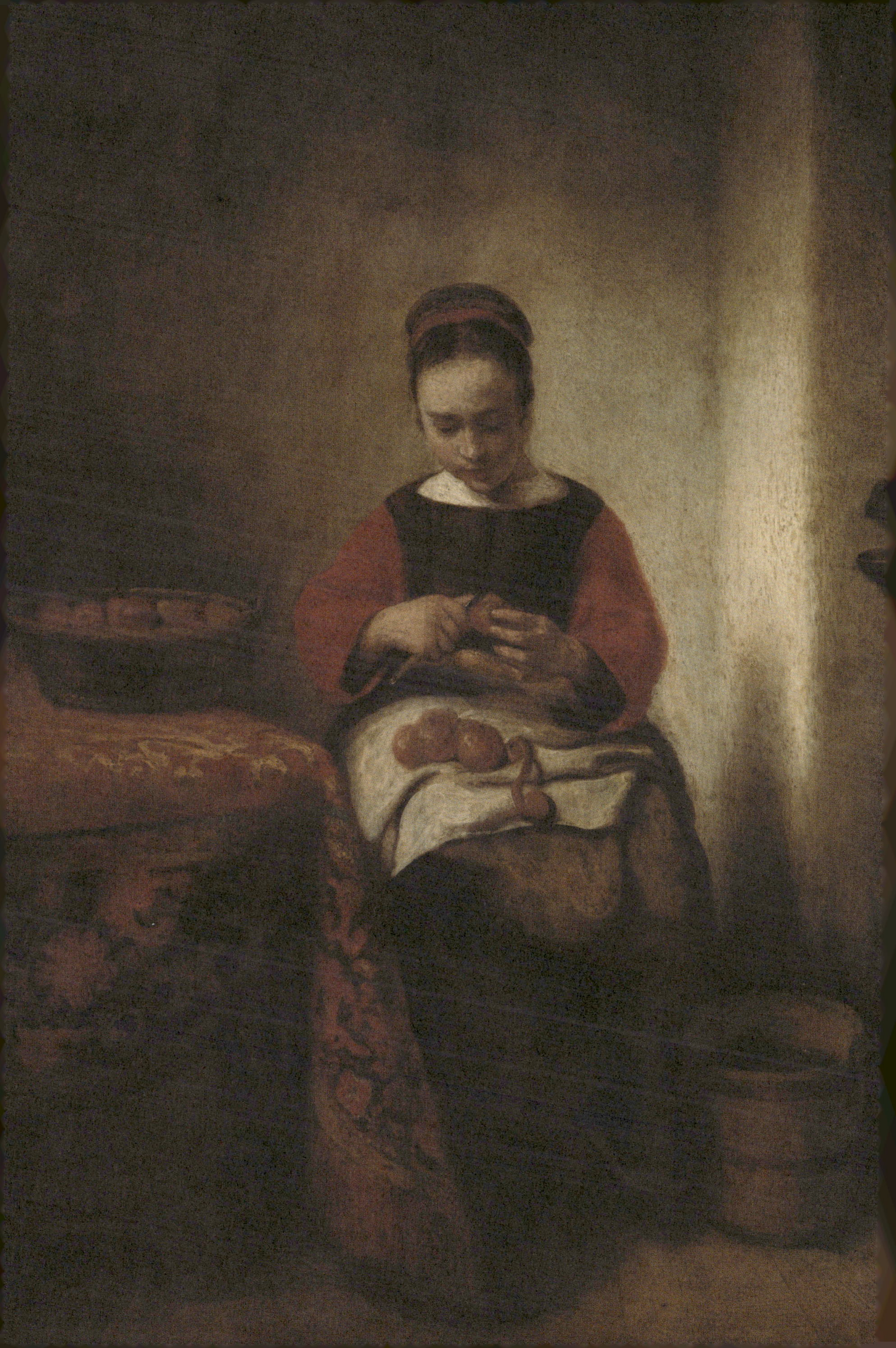

To Autumn

This poem belongs to a classical genre known as the ode—a lyric poem written in an exalted style. Like most odes, this one is a celebration of its subject. "To Autumn" is *the* classic English poem on autumn and harvest. It was composed on a Sunday in September of 1819 after John Keats had taken a walk in the water meadows around Winchester Cathedral. It is the last great poem written by Keats, who died of tuberculosis at the age of twenty-five.

Although it is packed with poetic technique, we can assimilate this poem at whatever level of complexity we wish. We need to begin, however, with what C. S. Lewis called "the central, obvious appeal of a great work." At the broadest level, "To Autumn" is a collection of pleasing snapshots of the autumn season—a catalog of the sights and sounds of a season of the year. The poem calls our attention to two key aspects of autumn: its beauty and its role as the climax to the summer growing season. It also uses the technique of personification, as Keats addresses the season directly in the mode of *apostrophe*. We experience autumn through this poem as a presiding presence who carries out a grand enterprise.

If we choose to explore the poem's technical intricacies, we will find that it moves in sequences from one stanza to the next. As we read, we progress from the maturing of late summer, to harvest ripeness, and finally to an anticipation of winter after the harvest. At the sensory level, we move from touch to sight to sound. The agents of each stanza's activity change from vegetable to human to animal. Three different aspects of harvest also successively appear throughout the stanzas: its fruitfulness, its labor, and its decline. The stanzas also take us through the daily cycle of morning to midday to evening.

As our representative, Keats says and pictures what we too feel and cherish about the autumn season. As the poem observes and celebrates autumn and harvest, we can assimilate it as a thanksgiving poem as well, using it to express our thanks to God for all that it portrays. ∎

Psalm 67:6 captures the spirit in which a Christian experiences this poem and the harvest season itself: "The earth has yielded its increase; God, our God, shall bless us."

previous: Nicolaes Maes, *Young Woman Peeling Apples*, ca. 1655
this page: Jean-François Millet; *Autumn Landscape with a Flock of Turkeys*, 1872–73

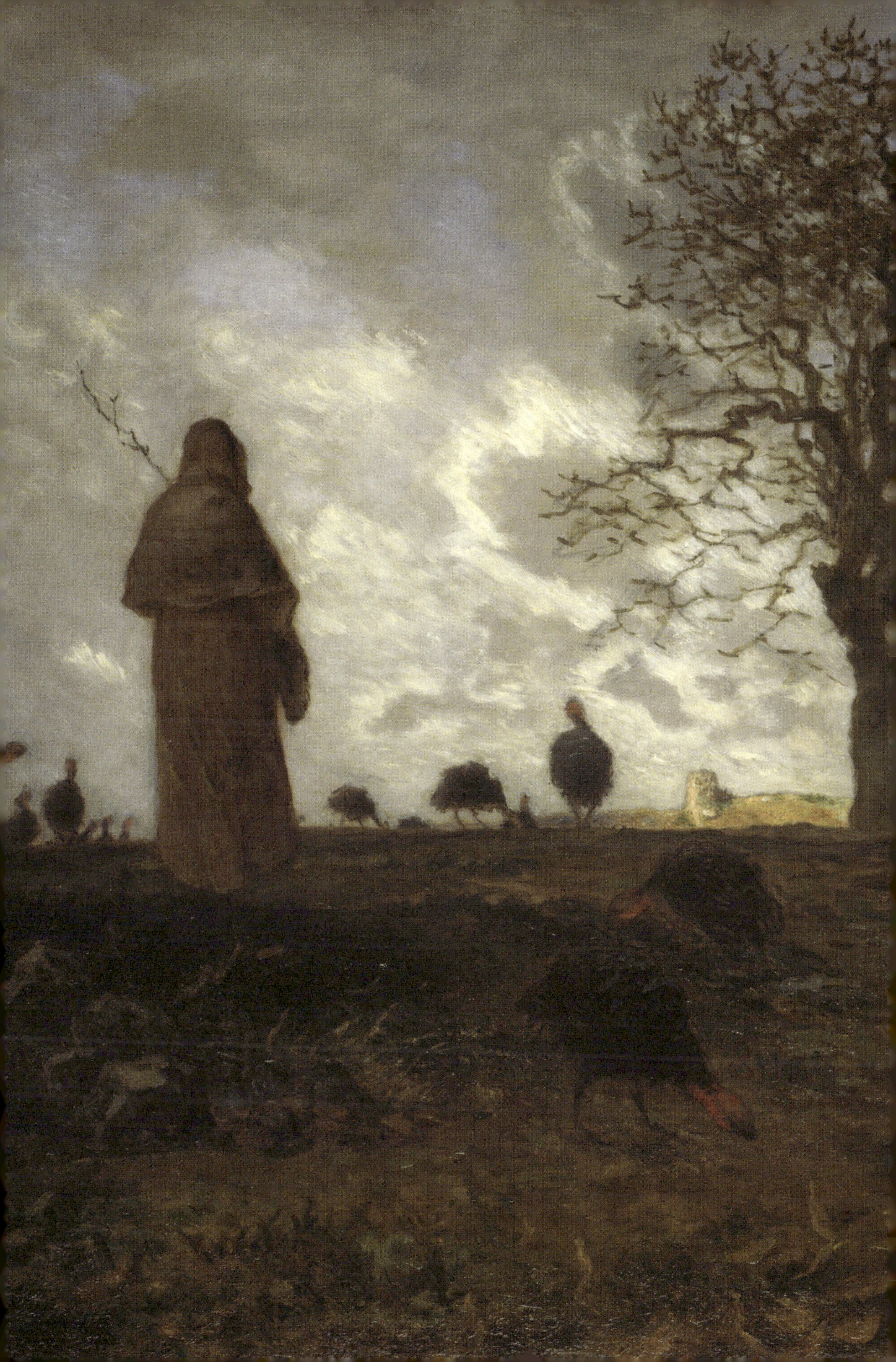

Puritan Reflections on Nature as a Revelation of God

Thomas Shepherd (1605–1649), Thomas Taylor (1576–1632), and Richard Baxter (1615–1691)

The Sincere Convert, 1664

When we see a stately house, although we see not the man that built it, although also we know not the time when it was built, yet will we conclude that surely some wise artificer has been working here. Can we, when we behold the stately theater of heaven and earth, conclude other but that the finger, arms, and wisdom of God have been here, although we see not him that is invisible, and although we know not the time when he began to build?

Every creature in heaven and earth is a loud preacher of this truth. Who set those candles, those torches of heaven, on the table? Who hung out those lanterns in heaven to enlighten a dark world? Who can make the statue of a man, but one wiser than the stone out of which it is hewn? Could any frame a man but one wiser and greater than man? Who taught the birds to build their nests, and the bees to set up and order their commonwealth? Who sends the sun [as a postage carrier] from one end of heaven to the other, carrying so many thousand blessings to so many thousands of people and kingdoms? What power of man or angels can make the least pile of grass, or put life into the least fly, if once dead? There is, therefore, a power above all created power, which is God.

A Man in Christ, 1635

THE CREATION OF THE WORLD is a Scripture of God, and the voice of God in all the creatures, and by them all speaks unto us always and everywhere. The whole world is his book, with as many pages as there are . . . creatures. No page is empty, but full of lines. Every quality of the creature is a . . . letter [of the alphabet] of these lines, and no letter without a part of God's wisdom in it.

"The Catechising of Families," 1682

WHEN WE LOOK on or think of the incomprehensible glory of the sun, its wonderful greatness, motion, light, and quickening heat; of the multitude and magnitude of the glorious stars; of the vast heavenly regions, the incomprehensible invisible spirits of powers that actuate and rule them all; when we come downward and think of the air and its inhabitants, and of this earth, a vast body to us, but as one inch or point in the whole creation; of the many nations, animals, plants of wonderful variety, the terrible depths of the ocean, and its numerous inhabitants. . . . All these must be to us but as the [window] that shows somewhat of the face of God, or as the letters of this great book, of which God is the sense, or as the actions of a living body by which the invisible soul is known. And as we study arts for our physical use, we must study the whole world, even the works of God, to this purposed use, that we may see, love, reverence, and admire God in all.

To say that nature is God's revelation to humanity encompasses three distinct ideas. One is that nature reveals something that would otherwise be hidden. Upon reflection, we can discern multiple things that nature *reveals* to us, but before we pursue this line of thought, we should identify the other two ideas.

The second is that God is the author or origin of nature and, therefore, the author or origin of what it reveals to us. Nature is God's possession by virtue of his creation of it and his providence over it. The revelation that we receive from nature is therefore a message from God.

But the most subtle the most subtle of these three ideas is that God himself is revealed in nature. By way of parallel, the opening verse of Revelation announces that the subject of the book is "the revelation of Jesus Christ." In the pages that follow, Jesus stands revealed in his nature and worthiness. So too nature is not only a revelation *from* God but a revelation *of* him. If we contemplate nature correctly, we see God.

All of this is implied in these passages from three towering Puritans. And yet, if the authors had simply asserted these truths using abstract vocabulary, their remarks would be relegated to a theology book instead of appearing in a stirring entry in a devotional anthology. The passages are infused by two literary techniques: metaphor and description.

The authors use metaphors to activate our imagination and prompt us to reflection. For example, nature is a *stately house* and *theater*. Every creature is a *loud preacher*. Nature is also a *book*—in fact, a *Scripture*. The agents and forces of nature are a *window* that shows the *face of God*. Metaphors like these require us to *carry over* (the literal definition of *metaphor*) meaning from one area of our experience to another in order to shed light on it. The descriptive imagination is equally prominent in these selections. It comes out in the lists of specific flora and fauna, so that we take an imaginative stroll in a park as we read them. But these appeals to our imagination never make us lose sight of what nature is revealing—the character of God—nor its goal in doing so: *that we may see, love, reverence, and admire God in all*.

These Puritan authors have given us an assignment. As we ponder the specific things about God that are revealed through nature, we can unpack the meanings embodied in the metaphors that permeate these passages. ■

One of the Old Testament nature psalms asserts the same truths these Puritan authors hold before us. Through the agency of nature, it tells us, "day to day pours out speech, and night to night reveals knowledge.... Their voice goes out through all the earth, and their words to the end of the world" (Ps. 19:2, 4).

previous: John William Casilear, *Lake George*, after 1851
this page: Joris Hoefnagel, *Hairy Dragonfly and Two Darters; Moth and Butterfly with Other Insects and a Columbine Flower*, ca. 1575/1580

How Nature Illuminates Godliness

Selections from Psalms and Proverbs

[The godly person] is like a tree
   planted by streams of water
that yields its fruit in its season,
   and its leaf does not wither.

I am like a green olive tree
   in the house of God.

The righteous flourish like the palm tree
   and grow like a cedar in Lebanon.
They are planted in the house of the Lord;
   they flourish in the courts of our God.
They still bear fruit in old age;
   they are ever full of sap and green.

Those who trust in the Lord are like Mount Zion,
   which cannot be moved, but abides forever.
As the mountains surround Jerusalem,
   so the Lord surrounds his people.

Blessed is everyone who fears the Lord,
   who walks in his ways.
Your wife will be like a fruitful vine
   within your house;
your children will be like olive shoots
   around your table.

The path of the righteous is like the light of dawn,
   which shines brighter and brighter until full day.

How Nature Illuminates Godliness

The quotations that comprise this entry give us a string of analogies in the form of metaphors and similes. This is no surprise, because nature is our single greatest source of metaphors.

Metaphors and similes are bifocal. They assert that A is like B. *B* is the actual subject of the statement—godliness, for example. *A* is the image (such as a fruitful tree) or the sphere of life that is being used to shed light on that subject. For this transaction to work, we need to fully experience level A of the comparison. Only when we experience this level are we in a position to carry over the meanings to the second half of the analogy. In this regard, it is useful to know that the word *metaphor* is based on Greek and Latin words meaning "to carry over." We need to avoid dismissing level A simply because the actual subject is level B. Being put in touch with human experience at level A is a bonus that poetry is always springing on us.

These considerations open the door to our experiencing this entry's printed passages from Psalms and Proverbs as both nature writing and a portrait of the godly person. We start with the images from nature. If we segregate them by themselves, we find that they function just as we expect nature writing to function. They present for our contemplation archetypes of nature that speak deeply to our psyche and our emotional being. An easy proof of this is to note that the snapshots from nature in the passages correspond to the paintings that we hang on our walls or choose to view in our leisure time.

When we categorize the images that we find in the units, we see their theme more concretely. Here is the list: trees full of life and possessing lush, green leaves; mountains towering above a city; streams flowing with life-giving water. These are feel-good pictures of nature. Similarly, viewing the progress of the summer sun from sunrise to fullness at noon is one of the pleasures of life. The references to a *way* or *path* belong to the realm of nature because, in the Bible and elsewhere, walking down a pathway is understood to occur in a natural setting, as distinct from urban images of roads and streets. In summary, if we first concentrate on the images from nature (level A of the metaphors and similes), we will have a rich experience of nature poetry, with its usual reminders of moments of beauty and provision from nature and effect of awakening our longing for them.

But of course the actual subject of the quotations is a person who lives a godly life. Having fully experienced the nature images and analyzed their meanings, we need to carry over the meanings that apply to this subject.

Carrying over the meanings as described will yield the takeaway for this entry. This requires a "slow read," as we take time to explore the dimensions of the nature images, then identify the corresponding dimensions of godliness. Making the connection unlocks new angles of vision on both nature and godliness. ■

Like the passages in this entry, Jesus' promise in John 7:38 uses nature to shed light on the life of faith, and it can be regarded as a Christological fulfillment of Old Testament foreshadowings: "Whoever believes in me, as the Scripture has said, 'Out of his heart will flow rivers of living water.'"

previous: John Singer Sargent, *Olive Trees, Corfu*, 1909
this page: William Trost Richards, *Beach at Long Branch: Sunrise*, 1872

Lines Written in Early Spring

William Wordsworth (1770-1850)

I heard a thousand blended notes,
While in a grove I sat reclined,
In that sweet mood when pleasant thoughts
Bring sad thoughts to the mind.

To her fair works did nature link
The human soul that through me ran,
And much it grieved my heart to think
What man has made of man.

Through primrose tufts, in that green bower,
The periwinkle trailed its wreaths;
And 'tis my faith that every flower
Enjoys the air it breathes.

The birds around me hopped and played,
Their thoughts I cannot measure,
But the least motion which they made
It seemed a thrill of pleasure.

The budding twigs spread out their fan,
To catch the breezy air;
And I must think, do all I can,
That there was pleasure there.

If this belief from heaven be sent,
If such be Nature's holy plan,
Have I not reason to lament
What man has made of man?

Lines Written in Early Spring

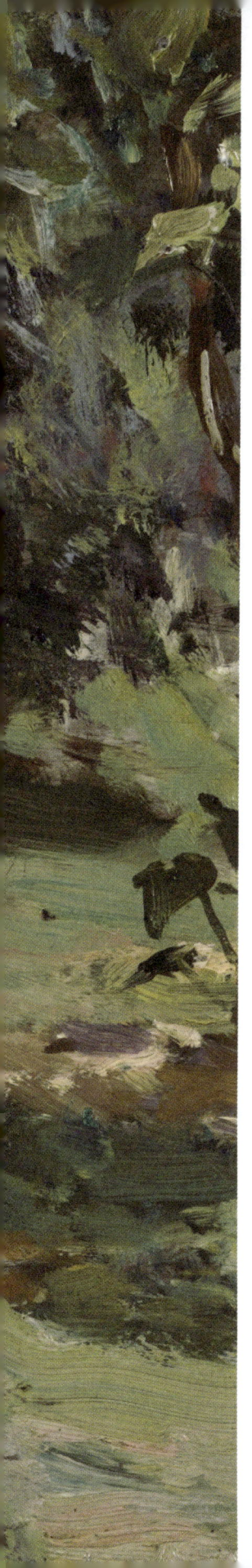

BRIEF SNAPSHOTS OF SPECIFIC FACETS OF NATURE—butterflies, daisies, rain, a robin in the backyard, and such—are a staple of nature-poem anthologies. Such snippets remain at an observational level and lack devotional potential. Substantial nature poems, however, add an element of interpretation to their observations of nature. Those that do so are known as descriptive-meditative poems. William Wordsworth's classic poem about his solitary excursion into the woods on an early spring day highlights the dynamics of such meditative nature poems.

Classic nature poems typically begin by situating their speaker in a natural setting. The opening stanza of "Lines Written in Early Spring" places the speaker in a woods in springtime, where he first experiences the scene in terms of its sounds. But the experience is as much mental as it is sensory, as the first stanza already signals through its references to *mood*, *thoughts*, and *mind*.

Nature poets almost always convey a sense of the unity of nature, including the kinship of people with nature, and Wordsworth quickly sets about doing this. His opening stanza portrays the diverse sounds of nature as a musical harmony of *blended notes*. In a similar fashion, the second stanza links the speaker's soul to the nature around him. Stanzas 3–5 elaborate on this motif of unity by using the imagery of periwinkle wreaths that *trail*, or interweave themselves, among *primrose tufts* and twigs that *spread out . . . to catch the breezy air*. Wordsworth also attributes human qualities to forces of nature in order to further connect them: flowers that breathe and birds that play and engage in deep thoughts. Then, having firmly established that these plants and birds enjoy themselves and experience *pleasure*, Wordsworth is ready to draw a religious conclusion from his immersion in springtime nature.

Although this religious message is concentrated within the last stanza, it is foreshadowed earlier in the poem. The speaker's *soul* is activated in the second

Irving Ramsey Wiles, *Spring Woods*, ca. 1900–20

71

stanza, and he affirms his *faith* in the next one. Religious vocabulary ultimately explodes in the final stanza, as it references *belief*, *heaven* (which through the centuries has been a metonymy, or substitution, for the word *God*), and a *holy plan*. Furthermore, Wordsworth's capitalization of *Nature* is meant to invoke God. The religious theme of the poem is twofold: good news about the perfection of Nature, and bad news about human sinfulness. The aphoristic phrase that Wordsworth twice uses to refer to the latter, *what man has made of man*, has become a permanent part of our storehouse of evocative sayings.

Wordsworth's poem subtly outlines an action plan for us to undertake. That plan is for us (1) to renew our commitment to experiencing and emulating nature, and, having been appropriately chastised, (2) to repent of the damage that human sinfulness has brought into the world. ■

The theological underpinning of Wordsworth's poem is that God created the natural order good but that, after the fall, the human race has done terrible things to itself (which is what the phrase *what man* [all humanity] *has made of man* means). A cryptic verse in Ecclesiastes asserts this in kernel form: "God made people good, but they have found all kinds of ways to be bad" (7:29 NCV).

William Langson Lathrop, *Spring Landscape*, ca. 1915

Virtue

George Herbert (1593–1633)

Sweet day, so cool, so calm, so bright,
The bridal of the earth and sky,
The dew shall weep thy fall tonight;
   For thou must die.

Sweet rose, whose hue angry and brave
Bids the rash gazer wipe his eye,
Thy root is ever in its grave,
   And thou must die.

Sweet spring, full of sweet days and roses,
A box where sweets compacted lie,
My music shows ye have your closes,
   And all must die.

Only a sweet and virtuous soul,
Like seasoned timber, never gives;
But though the whole world turn to coal,
   Then chiefly lives.

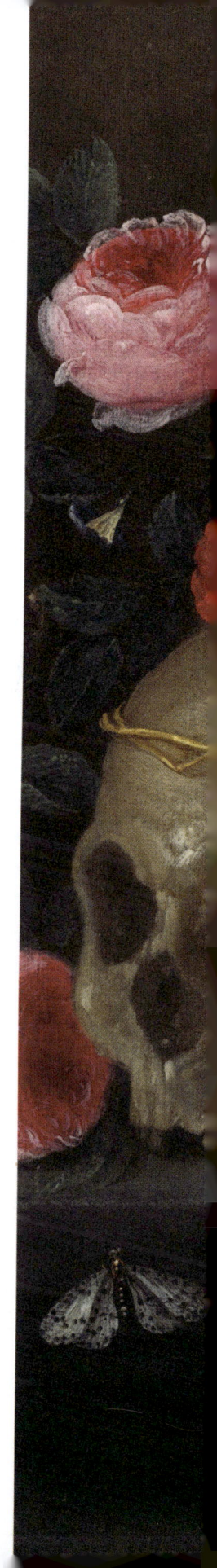

Virtue

On a first reading, this poem wins us with its simplicity. We see at a glance that it consists of four discreet stanzas that rhyme *abab*. Each stanza names a separate object: a spring day, a rose, a spring season, and a virtuous soul. Each of these is analyzed in terms of its final destination: death for the first three and, for the last, eternal life.

The first three stanzas can be enjoyed as a self-contained nature poem. We are led to luxuriate on certain qualities that are characteristic of a spring day, of a rose, and then of an entire spring season. The first two lines of each stanza paint a positive picture, while the concluding two turn that positive celebration into a lament over the transience of nature. The overall result is that of a eulogy—a remembrance of nature's beauty combined with sadness over the impermanence of that beauty. Three of nature's "best" make a bid for immortality and come up short. In effect, we witness a process of elimination in which a search for immortality is finally achieved after three failures.

These simple aspects of the text give way to complexity as we move from the mini-nature poem of the first three stanzas to contemplate the work as a whole. As we assimilate the last stanza, it dawns on us that the primary subject of the poem is not nature but the immortality of the Christian's soul. Now we can see that the poem as a whole makes use of the rhetorical technique known as a *foil*—something that often highlights a work's real subject by means of contrast, just as a gold setting enhances a jewel. Does this prompt us to disparage nature? Not at all. By way of parallel, the hymn "Fairest Lord Jesus" evokes such nature images as meadows, woodlands, and "the blooming garb of spring," only to declare that Jesus is even more beautiful. The elevation of the ultimate subject of these poems depends on the worthiness of nature as a point of reference and comparison.

A final aspect of artistry in this ostensibly simple poem is the element of symmetry. Each line of its four stanzas is parallel to the corresponding line within the others. Line 1 of each stanza names a conventional poetic subject and declares it to be *sweet*, and the next line describes that subject further. The third line then delivers a message of doom. The final line announces a prophecy—three of them indicating death and one indicating life.

This poem can be applied in two clear ways: its first three stanzas remind us how much we value the beauty of nature and lament its transience at the end of the spring season, and its final stanza leads us to embrace our hope of being glorified in heaven on the last day. ■

George Herbert's poem is built on what literary scholars call a biblical subtext: "The world is passing away..., but whoever does the will of God abides forever" (1 John 2:17).

Jan van Kessel the Elder,
Vanitas Still Life, ca. 1665/1670

Great Moments of Epiphany in Nature

William Cullen Bryant (1794–1878), Sidney Lanier (1842–1881), Charles Dickens (1812–1870), and Alfred, Lord Tennyson (1809–1892)

"To a Waterfowl"

He who from zone to zone
Guides through the boundless sky thy certain flight,
In the long way that I must trace alone,
Will lead my steps aright.

"The Marshes of Glynn"

As the marsh-hen secretly builds on the watery sod,
Behold I will build me a nest on the greatness of God.
I will fly in the greatness of God as the marsh-hen flies
In the freedom that fills all the space 'twixt the marsh and the skies.
By so many roots as the marsh-grass sends in the sod
I will heartily lay me ahold on the greatness of God.
Oh, like to the greatness of God is the greatness within
The range of the marshes, the liberal marshes of Glynn.

Great Expectations, 1861

THE JUNE WEATHER WAS DELICIOUS. The sky was blue, the larks were soaring high over the green corn, I thought all that countryside more beautiful and peaceful by far than I had ever known it to be yet. Many pleasant pictures of the life that I would lead there, and of the change for the better that would come over my character when I had a guiding spirit at my side whose simple faith and clear home wisdom I had proved, beguiled my way. They awakened a tender emotion in me; for my heart was softened by my return, and such a change had come to pass, that I felt like one who was toiling home barefoot from distant travel, and whose wanderings had lasted many years.

"Homage to Christ from Modern Magi," 1899

A VISITOR OF THE POET ventured to ask him what he thought of our Lord Jesus Christ. They were walking in the garden, and for a minute Tennyson said nothing; then he stopped by some beautiful flower, and said simply, "What the sun is to that flower Jesus Christ is to my soul. He is the sun of my soul." ∎

Great Moments of Epiphany in Nature

John Frederick Kensett, *October in the Marshes*, 1872

The word *epiphany* means a "sudden revelation or insight." As used by literary scholars, a moment of epiphany is a place late in a story or poem that reveals the main insight of the work and explicitly states it for characters in the work as well as for readers. Real life provides moments of epiphany as well. English nature poet William Wordsworth spoke of "spots of time" in our lives—memories of high points of insight, tied to a specific time and place, that we return to with restorative effect throughout our lives. In fact, he claimed that such moments are "scattered everywhere." The four passages that comprise this entry are spots of time drawn from the realm of literature.

At the age of twenty-one, William Cullen Bryant was walking from one New England town to another. As night fell, he observed a bird in flight and surmised that it was headed for a resting place on the marshy shore of a nearby lake. At that moment, Bryant experienced an epiphany as he realized that God's providence, which was directing the bird, could also be trusted to guide him during a critical time in his young life. In the climactic last stanza of the poem that this experience inspired—the stanza

Great Moments of Epiphany in Nature

included in this entry—he draws an analogy between the waterfowl and himself.

American poet Sidney Lanier wrote a whole volume of poems titled *Hymns of the Marshes*, which celebrates the salt marshes of coastal Georgia. These poems combine descriptions of nature with religious testimony. One day, a moment of spiritual insight struck the poet as he saw how his beloved marshland provided pictures of *the greatness of God*—a phrase that appears four times in the famous stanza of the poem that appears here. As the poet turns the prism in the light, specific features of the marshy scene reveal various aspects of the greatness of God.

The third passage occurs late in Charles Dickens's masterpiece *Great Expectations*. Its protagonist and narrator is a prodigal who is returning to the hometown where he was raised. He has repudiated a city life that was based on the false values of affluence and has embraced the humble life of his upbringing. Yet his description of nature and its accompanying emotions can be easily detached from this immediate narrative context, so that the beauty of his descriptions and his affective vocabulary can serve to uplift our spirits in a celebration of the benevolence of God and the beauty of language.

The anecdote involving Alfred, Lord Tennyson, a poet laureate of England, describes his moment of epiphany in a garden. The evocative metaphor of Jesus being the sun of one's soul is justly famous in Christian circles. In fact, a contemporary of Tennyson's, the Victorian John Henry Newman, wrote a familiar hymn titled "Sun of My Soul."

Literary epiphanies happen to specific characters in a poem or story, but, as C. S. Lewis argued, the particulars of literature are a net that captures the universal. Since this is the case, we can make these four passages' moments of insight our own. ■

The most famous epiphany evoked by nature appears in the book of Job and consists of God's speeches from the whirlwind and Job's responses to them. After God has presented him with nature's evidence of God's superior power and knowledge, Job responds with a newly felt humility as he suddenly grasps the supreme greatness of God: "Behold, I am of small account; what shall I answer you?" (Job 40:4)

Day Is Dying in the West

MARY LATHBURY (1841–1913)

Day is dying in the west;
Heav'n is touching earth with rest;
Wait and worship while the night
Sets her evening lamps alight
Through all the sky.

Lord of life, beneath the dome
Of the universe, Thy home,
Gather us who seek Thy face
To the fold of Thy embrace,
For Thou art nigh.

While the deepening shadows fall,
Heart of Love, enfolding all,
Through the glory and the grace
Of the stars that veil Thy face,
Our hearts ascend.

When forever from our sight
Pass the stars, the day, the night,
Lord of angels, on our eyes
Let eternal morning rise,
And shadows end.

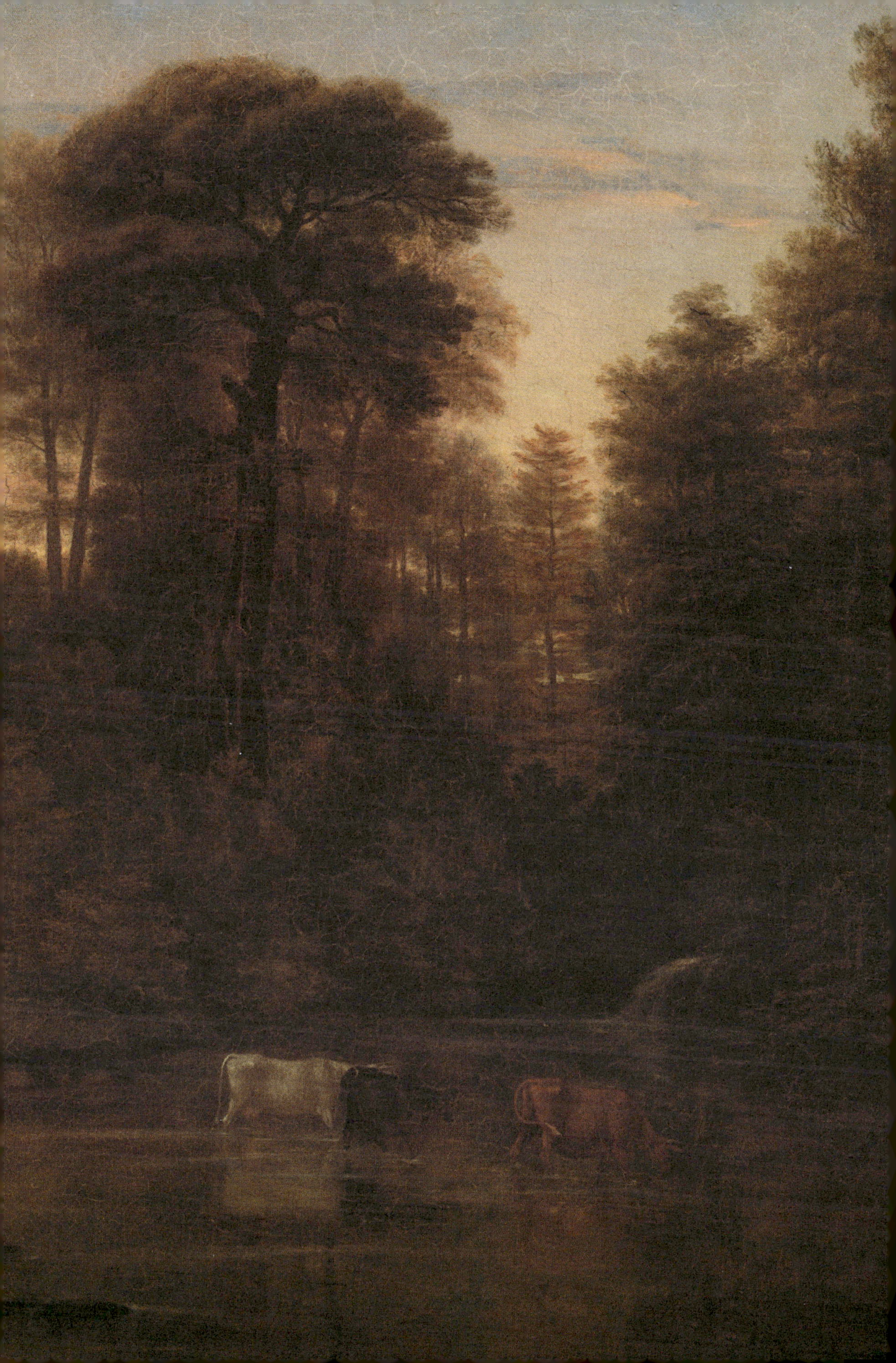

NATURE IS READILY AVAILABLE TO US—found on our very doorstep or seen from our living room window. Although many encounters with nature may feel ordinary, a few stand out as extraordinary. A camp experience, family vacation, or trips to a park or place of scenic beauty serve to heighten our senses, and our openness to nature, by setting us apart from our familiar neighborhoods. "Day Is Dying in the West" originated as a poem written for such a setting. The author, Mary Lathbury, was the poet laureate of Lake Chautauqua in New York—a Methodist camp and Bible study institute that began in 1874 and continues to the present day. She wrote this hymn for use at the evening services at the camp.

The Romantic movement of the early nineteenth century, which has influenced every poet since, contains a specific genre of nature poetry known as the evening poem. In contrast to the exuberance of sunrise, which gives the impression that energy has infused the world and given things a fresh start, twilight and nightfall suggest that things are shutting down and bringing closure—a phenomenon that a literary scholar has discussed in a book with the evocative title *The Invention of Evening*. "Day Is Dying in the West" follows this evening-poem tradition by capturing that same somber twilight atmosphere.

This is a devotional poem as well as a nature poem, yet we need to begin by analyzing it at the nature level, since that is the foundation on which the poet builds her thoughts and feelings. Its opening stanza immerses us in the physical details of nightfall, which it describes in exalted terms. Stanza 2 advances our awareness of nightfall by picturing the darkening sky as a vast *dome* over us. The next stanza offers a picture of stars functioning as a *veil* behind which God resides. In the last stanza, the poem taps into a familiar hymnic convention known as the eschatological turn—a shift of focus to the afterlife—as it leads us to contemplate our eventual passage from night into the dawn of *eternal morning*. The entire work represents mood poetry at its best, through its evocative images such as *dying* day, fading light, *deepening shadows*, the *embrace* of night, and *stars that veil*.

Part of the brilliance of this poem lies with its organization, which causes it to flow seamlessly from stanza to stanza. The other part of its beauty stems from its imagery and metaphors. For example, nightfall is portrayed as a metaphoric death of the day. The sun on the western horizon touches the earth. And stars are lamps hung throughout the sky. The poem holds together all the more because of several image patterns woven

previous: Washington Allston,
A Landscape after Sunset, ca. 1819

throughout it, such as light and dark, enfolding or surrounding, stars, and the vertical imagery of ascending and looking upward. A devotional overlay emerges from the second and fourth stanzas, which are phrased as prayers to God.

We can use this poem to express our own experiences of nightfall and evening and as a guide to give us an expanded conception of the emotional and spiritual potential of nature at the end of a day. ■

"Day Is Dying in the West" is an evening song that ties into evening worship as practiced in Bible times. Psalm 42:8 parallels Lathbury's vesper hymn: "By day the Lord commands his steadfast love, and at night his song is with me, a prayer to the God of my life."

Théodore Rousseau, *Sunset near Arbonne*, ca. 1860–65

How Nature Is Always Changing

Ralph Waldo Emerson (1803–1882)

The first in time and the first in importance of the influences upon the mind is that of nature. Every day, the sun; and, after sunset, night and her stars. Ever the winds blow; ever the grass grows. Every day, men and women, conversing, beholding and beholden.... There is never a beginning, there is never an end, to the inexplicable continuity of this web of God....

To the attentive eye, each moment of the year has its own beauty, and in the same field, it beholds, every hour, a picture which was never seen before, and which shall never be seen again. The heavens change every moment, and reflect their glory or gloom on the plains beneath. The state of the crop in the surrounding farms alters the expression of the earth from week to week. The succession of native plants in the pastures and roadsides, which makes the silent clock by which time tells the summer hours, will make even the divisions of the day sensible to a keen observer. The tribes of birds and insects, like the plants punctual to their time, follow each other, and the year has room for all. By water-courses, the variety is greater.... Art cannot rival this pomp.... The river is a perpetual gala, and boasts each month a new ornament....

Not the sun or the summer alone, but every hour and season yields its tribute of delight; for every hour and change corresponds to and authorizes a different state of the mind, from breathless noon to grimmest midnight.... Within the plantations of God [the woods], a decorum and sanctity reign, a perennial festival is dressed, and the guest sees not how he should tire of them in a thousand years.... Man is surprised to find that things near are not less beautiful and wondrous than things remote. The near explains the far. The drop is a small ocean.

Nature satisfies the soul purely by its loveliness.... I see the spectacle of morning from the hill-top over against my house, from daybreak to sunrise, with emotions which an angel might share. The long slender bars of cloud float like fishes in the sea of crimson light. From the earth, as a shore, I look out into that silent sea. I seem to partake its rapid transformations: the active enchantment reaches my dust, and I dilate and conspire with the morning wind. How does Nature exalt us with a few cheap elements!... The world lies no longer a dull miscellany and lumber-room, but has form and order. ■

MUCH ABOUT THE NATURE THAT SURROUNDS US makes it a touchstone for stability and permanence. After all, day after day we see constancy as we look out our windows, even though we are aware of seasonal changes. Poets have therefore turned to nature as a symbol of permanence—such as when the psalmist compares "those who trust in the LORD" to "Mount Zion, which cannot be moved, but abides forever" (Ps. 125:1). In this entry, however, Ralph Waldo Emerson, one of the great nature writers of American literature, alerts us to a complementary aspect of nature: the ways in which it is always changing. As we read Emerson's insights, we recognize that nature is not like a landscape painting or a photo but more like a video.

To demonstrate and convince us that nature is dynamic, Emerson uses the listing or catalog technique that is common in nature writing. He bombards us with sights from everyday life that are drawn from diverse spheres. The examples within the first paragraph focus on daily changes, such as the progress of the sun and the continuous movement of the wind. The second paragraph gives examples of seasonal changes. Then, in the third paragraph, as though he wants to make sure we do not miss a single pleasurable change of nature, Emerson champions those that take place throughout *every hour and season*. His list of examples is so extensive that we cannot help but agree with his argument that nature is in constant flux.

The passage is filled with so many metaphors and aphoristic turns of phrase that it ranks as a prose poem: the constant flow of natural changes it describes, for instance, is called a *web* being spun by God. A riverside that hosts a succession of plants and animals is a *perpetual gala* or dress-up party. Forests are the *plantations of God* and a *perennial festival* at which a human visitor is a *guest*. The sky above is like a *silent sea*, and its moving clouds are *like fishes*.

A lyric note of emotion and excitement infuses the poem. Emerson's vocabulary is in the superlative mode: *every* day, *each* moment, a *perpetual* gala, *every* hour and season, a *perennial* festival. Any *guest* witnessing this spectacle (including the reader) could not tire of its beauties *in a thousand years*, and as the speaker feels himself participating in nature's *rapid transformations* (a phrase that encapsulates the central theme of the entire passage), he is touched by the *active enchantment* of the experience.

From this passage, we should take away an inclination to observe the dynamic spectacle of ever-changing nature, and to gratefully receive it as a gift from God that prevents our daily routine from descending into a boring sameness. ∎

Emerson wishes not only to assert the fact of nature's ceaseless motion but also to prompt us to actually see it for ourselves. This reminds us of God's statement in Isaiah 43:19: "Behold, I am doing a new thing; . . . do you not perceive it?" Nature is one of the spheres in which God is perpetually "doing a new thing."

Friedrich Salathé, *Rays of Sunlight Striking a Woodland Path*, ca. 1815

Lines Written in Kensington Gardens

Matthew Arnold (1822–1888)

In this lone, open glade I lie,
Screen'd by deep boughs on either hand;
And at its end, to stay the eye,
Those black-crown'd, red-boled pine-trees stand!

Birds here make song, each bird has his,
Across the girdling city's hum.
How green under the boughs it is!
How thick the tremulous sheep-cries come!

Sometimes a child will cross the glade
To take his nurse his broken toy,
Sometimes a thrush flit overhead
Deep in her unknown day's employ.

Here at my feet what wonders pass,
What endless, active life is here!
What blowing daisies, fragrant grass!
An air-stirr'd forest, fresh and clear.

I, on men's impious uproar hurled,
Think often, as I hear them rave,
That peace has left the upper world
And now keeps only in the grave.

Yet here is peace for ever new!
When I who watch them am away,
Still all things in this glade go through
The changes of their quiet day.

Then to their happy rest they pass!
The flowers upclose, the birds are fed,
The night comes down upon the grass,
The child sleeps warmly in his bed.

Calm soul of all things! make it mine
To feel, amid the city's jar,
That there abides a peace of thine,
Man did not make, and cannot mar.

The will to neither strive nor cry,
The power to feel with others, give!
Calm, calm me more! nor let me die
Before I have begun to live.

Lines Written in Kensington Gardens

WRITTEN BY A TOWERING CULTURAL CRITIC of the Victorian age, this poem has all the traits of the Romantic nature poetry that William Wordsworth introduced half a century earlier: it celebrates nature, commends it to us, and contrasts its serenity with the madness of civilization. But while reenacting these familiar Romantic rituals, the poem springs a surprise on us: its outpouring of adoration for nature has its origin in a park at the heart of what was then the largest city in the world. Accordingly, this poem reminds us that nature can be found in urban settings too. However, the poem also develops an extended contrast between nature and civilization, as Arnold associates nature primarily with calmness and civilization with turmoil and striving.

Lines Written in Kensington Gardens

Arnold's poem belongs to the major Romantic genre known as the descriptive-meditative poem. Although many entries in that genre first describe nature and then move to a takeaway lesson at the end, this poem moves fluidly between observation and reflection and back again. In some of its stanzas, the poet recreates the specific sights and feelings that he experienced in Kensington Gardens. In others, he reflects on the meaning and personal application he derives from this moment in nature. The sensory experience of nature gives rise to his meditation and also validates the claims that the poet makes about nature. We should equally relish the poem's evocation of the pleasures of nature and the thoughts that these pleasures engender about the relative merits of nature and of civilization.

Following the back and forth movement between description and reflection, the poem's final two stanzas anchor the poem in meditation. In them, the poet apostrophizes nature—addresses it directly as though it were capable of hearing and responding—in a manner reminiscent of Robert Herrick's address to daffodils (see page 96) and John Keats's to autumn (see page 58). These stanzas are petitionary; though not a prayer addressed to God, they produce a similar effect. They are solemn in tone and elevated in language, which leads us to understand that what the poem has previously described is a momentous matter. They are an invitation for us to take seriously nature's effects on us and its potential for good in our lives.

We should apply this poem by allowing it to remind us of our pleasurable encounters with nature in urban settings and city parks. We should also embrace its commendation of the benefits of nature and heed its critique of the misguided values and lifestyle that civilization often engenders. ■

This poem's commendation of nature, and its warning against civilization's tendency to lure us into a frenzied lifestyle, are not simply the product of nineteenth-century Romanticism; they are also present in the Bible. Jesus, for example, taught us to "consider the lilies of the field, . . . [and] do not be anxious." (Matt. 6:28, 31).

previous: Joseph Pennell, *Kensington Gardens*, 1887
this page: Henri-Edmond Cross, *Landscape*, ca. 1904

Walking in Nature

SELECTIONS FROM THE SONG OF SOLOMON
AND JONATHAN EDWARDS (1703–1758)

Song of Solomon 2:10–13; 7:11–12

My beloved speaks and says to me:
"Arise, my love, my beautiful one,
　　and come away,
for behold, the winter is past;
　　the rain is over and gone.
The flowers appear on the earth,
　　the time of singing has come,
and the voice of the turtledove
　　is heard in our land.
The fig tree ripens its figs,
　　and the vines are in blossom;
　　they give forth fragrance.
Arise, my love, my beautiful one,
　　and come away.

Come, my beloved,
　　let us go out into the fields
　　and lodge in the villages;
let us go out early to the vineyards
　　and see whether the vines have budded,
whether the grape blossoms have opened
　　and the pomegranates are in bloom.

Personal Narrative, 1765

I walked abroad alone, in a solitary place in my father's pasture, for contemplation. And as I was walking there, and looking up on the sky and clouds, there came into my mind so sweet a sense of the glorious majesty and grace of God, that I know not how to express. I seemed to see them both in a sweet conjunction; majesty and meekness joined together; it was a sweet, and gentle, and holy majesty; and also a majestic meekness; an awful sweetness; a high, and great, and holy gentleness. . . .

Once, as I rode out into the woods for my health, in 1737, having alighted from my horse in a retired place, as my manner commonly has been, to walk for divine contemplation and prayer, I had a view that for me was extraordinary, of the glory of the Son of God, as Mediator between God and man, and his wonderful, great, full, pure and sweet grace and love, and meek and gentle condescension. . . .

I very frequently used to retire into a solitary place, on the banks of the Hudson River, at some distance from the city, for contemplation on divine things and secret converse with God; and had many sweet hours there. Sometimes Mr. Smith and I walked there together, to converse on the things of God. ■

NATURE GIVES THE HUMAN RACE a language for talking about subjects beyond itself. For example, although only a handful of the Old Testament psalms are nature poems, nature appears so abundantly as an aid to devotion in the Psalms that the Psalter continuously immerses us in nature. Love poets also use nature as a vehicle for writing about their chosen subjects. In literary circles, Shakespeare's romantic comedies are called his "forest comedies" and "green world comedies" because they take place in the same kind of world that we find in the Song of Solomon: an idealized world of forests and pastures.

This entry's lines from Song of Solomon belong to a genre known as the "pastoral invitation." The speaker in such poems invites his or her beloved to go for a walk in an idealized natural landscape—an invitation that signifies an offer of mutually fulfilling love and even a metaphoric proposal of marriage. This type of nature writing gives us an irresistibly idealized experience of nature's beauty and appeal. Meanwhile, the entry's paragraphs from Jonathan Edwards illustrate how nature can provide us with a vehicle for spiritual experience and insight. Even in childhood, Edwards made a practice of walking into the surrounding woods and building huts to pray.

Both works fall into the genre of walking, or peripatetic, literature that encourages us to *come away* from our homes to immerse ourselves in nature. Solomon's evocative invitation to *lodge in the villages* also communicates the journey away from civilization and into nature.

This entry's passages show how nature can serve a therapeutic function in our lives. Excursions into nature remove us temporarily from everyday life and then return us to it with a sense of renewed zest. One benefit of such an excursion is solitude—being away from people and society. While this may involve walking in nature by ourselves, these passages implicitly acknowledge that solitude in nature can be shared by two companions.

To apply this entry, we can answer the questions this discussion has raised. How might nature serve as an avenue for finding fulfillment alongside a beloved or friend? How can we use the excursions we take into nature to enhance our spiritual lives? How has walking in nature benefited our own psychic and emotional health? How do encounters with nature enrich our leisure and perhaps draw a boundary to protect us from the obligations of life? ■

The three primary strands that we see in this entry—romantic love, spiritual contemplation, and perambulation—converge in the endearing story of Isaac and Rebekah's first meeting:

> And Isaac went out to meditate in the field toward evening. And he lifted up his eyes and saw, and behold, there were camels coming. And Rebekah lifted up her eyes, and when she saw Isaac, she dismounted from the camel and said to the servant, "Who is that man, walking in the field to meet us?" (Gen. 24:63–65)

previous: Thomas Gainsborough, *Landscape with Rustic Lovers*, ca. 1755-1759;
John Callcott Horsley, *Lovers under a Blossom Tree*, by 1859

To Daffodils
Robert Herrick (1591–1674)

Fair daffodils, we weep to see
You haste away so soon;
As yet the early-rising sun
Has not attained his noon.
Stay, stay
Until the hasting day
Has run
But to the evensong;
And, having prayed together, we
Will go with you along.

We have short time to stay, as you;
We have as short a spring;
As quick a growth to meet decay,
As you, or anything.
We die
As your hours do, and dry
Away
Like to the summer's rain,
Or as the pearls of morning's dew,
Ne'er to be found again.

To Daffodils

IN EVERYDAY CONVERSATION, WE MIGHT OBSERVE, "It's sad that the daffodils have withered so quickly." In a mere twenty short lines, seventeenth-century cleric and poet Robert Herrick invests that commonplace observation with genuine insight and feeling. He deftly uses our longing for nature to remain perfect in order to awaken our longing for something that is eternal.

Herrick's central poetic maneuver is to address the daffodils in the technique known as apostrophe. In an act of sympathetic identification, the poet treats the daffodils with the tender affection that a parent feels for a small child. In the poem's first stanza, this sympathy takes the form of a lament. Its focus is one of the most prevalent themes of nature writing throughout the ages—flowers' fleeting beauty.

The poet's regret is accompanied by longing, another constant of nature writing. As we enter in spirit into the poet's lament over his beloved daffodils, we long for beauty, for life, for permanence, and for something that, while unnamed, is associated with transcendence. God has created us to long for something we cannot possess in this world, and not infrequently this longing is awakened by our golden moments in nature.

The poem's second stanza shifts from considering the daffodils to considering people, and its approach is intellectual and analytic rather than affective and emotional. Even after this shift of emphasis, however, the poem continues to be a nature poem as it leads us to picture the phenomena of the *spring* season and the drying up of the *summer's rain* and of the *pearls of morning's dew*. It shapes these facets of nature into a meditation on human mortality, which is something we understand with new clarity as it dawns on us that we are just like the daffodils—a *growth* that *meet[s] decay*. The poem drives this similarity home with the two words *as you*, which are addressed to the daffodils and appear twice in the stanza. In our vulnerability to death and decay, we are just like the daffodils.

This poem, which was written by an Anglican clergyman, contains just enough religious reference to prompt us toward spiritual application. It includes the words *evensong* and *prayed* as explicit references, but it becomes all the more effective by requiring us to supply a religious meaning. The poem informs us that we are headed for physical death, and then implicitly asks, "What are you going to do with this information?"

The takeaway is to open ourselves to all that the poem makes available to us: a longing for the beauty of nature, a regret that this beauty is fleeting, an awareness that we are just like the daffodils in our mortality, and a resolve to seek the permanence of the eternal world.

Psalm 90 covers the same territory as Herrick's poem, although it makes explicit the solution to the problem of nature's impermanence:

> Lord, you have been our dwelling place in all generations.... You return man to dust.... You sweep them away ... like grass that is renewed in the morning: in the morning it flourishes and is renewed; in the evening it fades and withers.... So teach us to number our days that we may get a heart of wisdom. (vv. 1, 3, 5–6, 12)

Herrick's meditation helps us to number our days and get a heart of wisdom in regard to our mortality.

previous: Suzuki Harunobu, *Birds and Narcissus*, ca. 1615–1868
this page: Zhu Ling, *Black Cat and Narcissus*, 1800s

How God Blesses Us through Nature

NATHANIEL HAWTHORNE (1804–1864)

I WENT OUT to walk about an hour ago, and found it very pleasant. . . . I went round and across the Common, and stood on the highest point of it, where I could see miles and miles into the country. Blessed be God for this green tract, and the view which it affords, whereby we poor citizens may be put in mind that all his earth is not composed of blocks of brick houses, and of stone or wooden pavements. Blessed be God for the sky, too. . . .

Life now swells and heaves beneath me like a brimful ocean; and the endeavor to comprise any portion of it in words is like trying to dip up the ocean in a goblet. . . . God bless and keep us! For there is something more awe-inspiring in happiness than in sorrow, the latter being earthly and finite, the former composed of the substance and texture of eternity, so that spirits still embodied may tremble at it. . . .

This is a glorious day—bright, very warm, yet with an unspeakable gentleness both in its warmth and brightness. On such days it is impossible not to love Nature, for she evidently loves us. At other seasons she does not give me this impression, or only at very rare intervals; but in these happy, autumnal days, when she has perfected the harvests, and accomplished every necessary thing that she had to do, she overflows with a blessed superfluity of love. It is good to be alive now. Thank God for breath—yes, for mere breath!—when it is made up of such a heavenly breeze as this. It comes to the cheek with a real kiss; it would linger fondly around us, if it might; but, since it must be gone, it caresses us with its whole kindly heart, and passes onward, to caress likewise the next thing it meets. There is a pervading blessing diffused over all the world. I look out of the window and think, "O perfect day! O beautiful world! O good God!" And such a day is the promise of a blissful eternity. Our Creator would never have made such weather, and given us the deep heart to enjoy it, above and beyond all thought, if he had not meant us to be immortal. It opens the gates of heaven and gives us glimpses far inward.

How God Blesses Us through Nature

THE OVERALL RHETORICAL STRATEGY IN this passage from Hawthorne's notebooks is all but inevitable in nature writing. That strategy is to combine description or observation with response. In the passage, we become Hawthorne's strolling companion as he walks on the village common and rises to a vantage point from which he can see the surrounding green landscape. We stand with him as he basks in the atmosphere of *autumnal days* and their *harvests*. We feel the caressing breeze as it passes by. The starting point for experiencing the fireworks of the passage is being put in touch with the earth as the earth really is.

But that is only its starting point. The glory of the passage is found in the emotional response of its speaker. It is a rapturous response that catches us up in its excitement. Exclamation marks are abundant, and yet even when the author chooses not to use them, the entire passage remains in an exclamatory mode. The speaker is chiefly ecstatic about nature's ability to instill in us a sense of well-being and optimism about life's possibilities. What do we desire on any given day more than to feel that *it is good to be alive*? Hawthorne masterfully portrays the relationship between us and nature as a reciprocal one. He repeatedly blesses nature; but, in a surprise move, he asserts not only that we love nature but that nature *evidently loves us*.

Rising beyond our interaction with nature is our interaction with God. In fact, the focus of the passage is solidly God-centered, much as we find in the Bible's own nature poetry. Furthermore, its whole orientation is doxological—it is aimed at praising God for his gift of nature. Thus we read such exclamations as *blessed be God for this green tract* of land, *blessed be God for the sky, thank God for breath,* and so forth. And not only do we bless God, but God uses nature to bestow a *pervading blessing diffused over all the world*. And in the climax of the passage, Hawthorne claims that nature is a signpost that points to what awaits us in heaven.

This uplifting passage has a double application. Certainly it gives expression to what we too wish to say at moments when nature works its healing effect on us. But there is a potential element of rebuke in Hawthorne's words as well. If nature can be all that the author records in this ecstatic passage, we can scarcely avoid feeling a need to "get with the program" and allow nature to be all that God intends it to be for us. ■

Hawthorne's ecstatic exclamations have three sources—his own inner sense of wellbeing, nature in its manifold forms, and the God who created both people and nature. Isaiah 42:5 brings these same three agents together as it speaks about "God, the Lord, who created the heavens and stretched them out, who spread out the earth and what comes from it, who gives breath to the people on it and spirit to those who walk in it."

Thomas Chambers, *The Connecticut Valley*, mid 1800s

I Sing the Mighty Power of God

Isaac Watts (1674–1748)

I sing the mighty power of God,
Who made the mountains rise,
Who spread the flowing seas abroad,
And built the lofty skies.

I sing the wisdom that ordained
The sun to rule the day;
The moon shines full at God's command,
And all the stars obey.

I sing the goodness of the Lord,
Who filled the earth with food,
Who formed the creatures by his Word,
And then pronounced them good.

Lord, how thy wonders are displayed,
Where'er I turn my eye,
When I survey the ground I tread,
Or gaze upon the sky.

There's not a plant or flower below,
But makes thy glories known;
And clouds arise, and tempests blow,
By order from thy throne.

All who receive their life from thee
Are subject to thy care;
There's not a place where we can flee
But God is present there.

I Sing the Mighty Power of God

Isaac Watts is known as the father of English hymnody because he freed English congregational hymns from their single-minded adherence to Psalm paraphrases. This hymnic poem, however, is so saturated with Old Testament subject matter and vocabulary that our first impulse may be to assume it is a paraphrase of a psalm anyway. It is, instead, a mosaic of references to many biblical passages. In addition, we may be surprised to learn that this demanding hymn was composed specifically for children.

We expect a nature poem to put us in touch with nature, and this hymn proves to be one by doing so—in fact, on a cosmic scale. Its imagery keeps us rooted in the world of nature from start to finish as it leads us to contemplate mountains, sea, sky, sun, moon, stars, animals, earth, plants, flowers, and clouds. It is not an overstatement to say that the poem ultimately serves as a concise summary of the theology that all Old Testament nature psalms put forth.

The comprehensiveness of the poem extends to its theology. Its theocentric focus is the first thing we notice. God is supremely elevated throughout, and nature provides the proof of his preeminence. God is the chief actor, and nature is the sphere of his actions. The poem leads us to contemplate a range of God's attributes that nature makes evident: namely, his *power* (stanza 1), *wisdom* (stanza 2), *goodness* (stanza 3), and omnipresence (stanzas 4–6). Then, as we take a step backward to survey the poem in its entirety, we can see that it exalts God for both creating nature and ruling over it providentially. Absorbing all of these details within the poem makes us feel as though it has said everything about its subject that can be said—and in only six concise stanzas.

What should we take away from Watts's hymnic poem? First, we ought to allow it to codify our understanding of God's character and his acts in nature. Second, we may ponder how this understanding should affect our dealings with him and with nature—the dual subjects of the hymn. ■

As the Israelites contributed toward the eventual building of the temple, David offered an exalted prayer that corroborates what Watts's hymn asserts: "Yours, O Lord, is the greatness and the power and the glory . . . , for all that is in the heavens and in the earth is yours" (1 Chron. 29:11).

Henry Golden Dearth, *Flecks of Foam*, ca. 1911/1912

Tintern Abbey

William Wordsworth (1770–1850)

Five years have past; five summers, with the length
Of five long winters! and again I hear
These waters, rolling from their mountain-springs
With a soft inland murmur. Once again
Do I behold these steep and lofty cliffs,
That on a wild secluded scene impress
Thoughts of more deep seclusion, and connect
The landscape with the quiet of the sky.
The day is come when I again repose
Here, under this dark sycamore, and view
These plots of cottage-ground, these orchard-tufts,
Which at this season, with their unripe fruits,
Are clad in one green hue, and lose themselves
'Mid groves and copses. Once again I see
These hedge-rows, hardly hedge-rows, little lines
Of sportive wood run wild: these pastoral farms,
Green to the very door. . . . .

          These beauteous forms,
Through a long absence, have not been to me
As is a landscape to a blind man's eye.
But oft, in lonely rooms, and 'mid the din
Of towns and cities, I have owed to them,
In hours of weariness, sensations sweet,
Felt in the blood, and felt along the heart,
And passing even into my purer mind
With tranquil restoration. . . . .

Tintern Abbey

. . . . How oft
In darkness and amid the many shapes
Of joyless daylight, when the fretful stir
Unprofitable, and the fever of the world,
Have hung upon the beatings of my heart—
How oft, in spirit, have I turned to thee,
O sylvan Wye! thou wanderer through the woods,
How often has my spirit turned to thee!
Knowing that nature never did betray
The heart that loved her; 'tis her privilege,
Through all the years of this our life, to lead
From joy to joy: for she can so inform
The mind that is within us, so impress
With quietness and beauty, and so feed
With lofty thoughts, that . . . .
. . . . not all
The dreary intercourse of daily life
Shall e'er prevail against us, or disturb
Our cheerful faith, that all which we behold
Is full of blessings. ■

THE POEM THAT APPEARS HERE is thoroughly autobiographical. Even though it is familiarly known as "Tintern Abbey," its published title was "Lines Composed a Few Miles above Tintern Abbey, On Revisiting the Banks of the Wye during a Tour. July 13, 1798." Wordsworth had visited the picturesque valley of the Wye River in Wales during a walking tour five years earlier. In the intervening years, he had suffered an emotional breakdown. "Tintern Abbey" recreates the sensations he experienced when he revisited the site, along with the thoughts that came to him as he sat in the same spot where he had sat five years before.

previous: J. Ashford, *Tintern Abbey*, 1820
this page: John "Warwick" Smith, *Tintern Abbey by Moonlight*, ca. 1789

Wordsworth devotes the poem's first stanza to the physical details of the place in which it was written. Tintern Abbey is not a cultivated park but a secluded, rustic place. It is a scene of quietude in which the poet allows himself to be absorbed into nature. In fact, it presents the archetypal green world—so much so that the farms and fencerows are indistinguishable from the surrounding trees and plants. Everything is dressed *in one green hue*.

Wordsworth's introspection brings him to several conclusions. The first is his grateful awareness of the fact that, during the five years since his earlier visit to the scene, he has been able to draw strength from memories of that visit. The primary gift that remembering this experience has brought him is emotional healing, which Wordsworth calls *tranquil restoration*. This healing effect of nature is one of Wordsworth's greatest themes and the governing theme of "Tintern Abbey." The poem's final stanza moves onward from the present and past to encompass the future as well, and its keynote is that nature can inspire a state of well-being in us and impart to us a *cheerful faith* that the world in which we live is benevolent and *full of blessings*.

After sharing in Wordsworth's experience and thinking, we can now follow his example. This poem belongs to a very large category of literature known as the "literature of place." We should allow it to register with us how important specific places are to our lives, especially certain places where we have had memorable encounters with nature. More specifically, the poem draws upon the motif of the place revisited. Inspired by Wordsworth's lines, we can use our re-visitation of places as an occasion to examine what has changed and what has remained constant in our lives. Finally, although we should resist the non-Christian tendency to claim too much for nature, we can recognize the accuracy of Wordsworth's claims that nature can serve as a beneficial influence on our moral and emotional lives and store up memories of specific places from which to draw strength after we have moved on. ■

Based on the personal encounter he had with a place of natural beauty, Wordsworth asserted his *cheerful faith that all which we behold is full of blessings*. This aligns with God's assessment of his creation of nature and people recorded in Genesis 1:31: "And God saw everything that he had made, and behold, it was very good."

The Snow Storm

Ralph Waldo Emerson (1803–1882)

Announced by all the trumpets of the sky,
Arrives the snow, and, driving o'er the fields,
Seems nowhere to alight; the whited air
Hides hill and woods, the river, and the heaven,
And veils the farmhouse at the garden's end.
The sled and traveler stopped, the courier's feet
Delayed, all friends shut out, the housemates sit
Around the radiant fireplace, enclosed
In a tumultuous privacy of storm.

Come see the north wind's masonry.
Out of an unseen quarry evermore
Furnished with tile, the fierce artificer
Curves his white bastions with projected roof
Round every windward stake, or tree, or door.
Speeding, the myriad-handed, his wild work
So fanciful, so savage, nought cares he
For number or proportion. Mockingly,
On coop or kennel he hangs Parian wreaths;
A swan-like form invests the hidden thorn;
Fills up the farmer's lane from wall to wall,
[Despite] the farmer's sighs; and at the gate
A tapering turret overtops the work.
And when his hours are numbered, and the world
Is all his own, retiring, as he were not,
Leaves, when the sun appears, astonished Art
To mimic in slow structures, stone by stone,
Built in an age, the mad wind's night-work,
The frolic architecture of the snow. ■

Emerson's poem is cut from the same cloth as nature passages we find in the Bible. One of these is Psalm 147:17, in which we read that God "hurls down his crystals of ice like crumbs; who can stand before his cold?"

As Emerson leads us to vicariously experience the snowstorm, we must note the poetic skill with which he makes the storm come alive in our imagination. Here it is useful to remind ourselves of how literature performs its feats. Literature places human experience before us for our contemplation. Because human experience is universal, at one level literature portrays what we already know. But it is the function of literature to present familiar experience in a new light by defamiliarizing it. English poet Samuel Taylor Coleridge asked rhetorically, "Who has not a thousand times seen snow fall on water? Who has not watched it *with a new feeling*" after reading a "poetic description of it?"

How does Emerson manage such a literary feat with a snowstorm? In his native New England during the nineteenth century, being snowbound was a common occurrence. Building on the foundation of the familiar, Emerson shows how the snowstorm transforms everyday objects—the woods, a river, a sled, a chicken coop, a lane, and so on—into an art gallery. His poem records the metamorphosis that a snowstorm, personified as a traveling artist and architect, works when it arrives, spends several hours preparing an art gallery, and then departs, leaving spectators to admire his work in stunned silence. Emerson thus emphasizes a fantastical element within the storm's artwork.

Although Emerson does not impose a religious meaning on the scene, a Christian reader familiar with the Bible, and especially the Psalms, will do so automatically. The snowstorm, for instance, is portrayed as possessing a sudden and paralyzing power that completely subdues people and halts their ordinary activities. The Bible similarly portrays God as controlling the forces of nature with superior power. Emerson's poem induces reverence for nature, just as the Bible induces reverence for both nature and the God of nature. The poem's specific details also remind us of the nature writing of Scripture. For example, Emerson pictures the snowstorm as having an unseen quarry from which it gathers its building materials, the way Job 38:22 similarly pictures God as having storehouses of snow and hail.

We can apply this poem by abandoning ourselves to our enjoyment of Emerson's poetic performance, and of the artistry of snowstorms, and to worship of the God whom the poem does not name but who is present to us in that very absence. ■

previous: Tom Ek, *Winter Forest after Snow Storm*, 2018

The Voice from the Whirlwind

Selections from Job 38

Where were you when I laid the foundation of the earth?
    Tell me, if you have understanding.
Who determined its measurements—surely you know!
    Or who stretched the line upon it?
On what were its bases sunk,
    or who laid its cornerstone,
when the morning stars sang together
    and all the sons of God shouted for joy?
Or who shut in the sea with doors
    when it burst out from the womb,
when I made clouds its garment
    and thick darkness its swaddling band,
and prescribed limits for it
    and set bars and doors,
and said, "Thus far shall you come, and no farther,
    and here shall your proud waves be stayed"?

Have you commanded the morning since your days began,
    and caused the dawn to know its place,
that it might take hold of the skirts of the earth,
    and the wicked be shaken out of it?

Have the gates of death been revealed to you,
    or have you seen the gates of deep darkness?
Have you comprehended the expanse of the earth?

Declare, if you know all this.
Where is the way to the dwelling of light,
    and where is the place of darkness,
that you may take it to its territory
    and that you may discern the paths to its home?

Have you entered the storehouses of the snow,
    or have you seen the storehouses of the hail,
which I have reserved for the time of trouble,
    for the day of battle and war?

Who has cleft a channel for the torrents of rain
    and a way for the thunderbolt,
to bring rain on a land where no man is,
    on the desert in which there is no man,
to satisfy the waste and desolate land,
    and to make the ground sprout with grass?
Has the rain a father,
    or who has begotten the drops of dew?

Can you lift up your voice to the clouds,
    that a flood of waters may cover you?
Can you send forth lightnings, that they may go
    and say to you, "Here we are"?

Who can number the clouds by wisdom?
    Or who can tilt the waterskins of the heavens,
when the dust runs into a mass
    and the clods stick fast together?

The Voice from the Whirlwind

WE WILL UNDERSTAND THIS POEM better if we place it into its context. When Job's good fortunes were taken from him, he responded to his suffering by accusing God of unfairness and malice, as summarized by God's eventual question to him, "Will you even put me in the wrong... and condemn me?" (Job 40:8). The poem printed above thus has the character of a rebuke to Job. Its purpose for Job and us is to instill humility before the God of nature.

Since the purpose of God's speech is to demonstrate his superior power over people and nature, it is no wonder that the poem portrays what literary scholars call the sublime, in contrast to the other tendency of nature writing called the picturesque. The forces of nature can be portrayed in either mode, and this poem specializes in the sublime. The three stanzas printed above, excerpted from a longer passage, cover three aspects of nature, stanza-by-stanza: the creation of the world at the beginning of time, the daily cycle of day and night, and weather in the specific form of the falling of precipitation.

The passage is a tour de force of poetry—an impressive performance that pushes the upper limit of the imagination's abilities. The key to seeing what is going on is to relish and unpack the comparisons that are present in the form of metaphors and similes. For example, God's artistry and careful planning in creating nature are compared to a builder who plans the dimensions and features of a building and then constructs its foundation. Clouds become an enclosing garment and blanket. Rain is imaginatively pictured as God's pouring it out of a kitchen water container. One byproduct is that the poem domesticates wonder, treating God's transcendent acts in nature in terms of commonplace everyday events, showing how easily God can perform his mighty feats in nature. Our response as we assimilate this is that we have never before viewed everyday nature in quite this way. We have a renewed admiration for poetry as well as nature.

In addition to being a poetic tour de force, the passage is also a rhetorical tour de force. For example, the passage consists of a continuous string of hammerlike rhetorical questions whose answer is self-evident. The purpose of these questions is not to elicit information but to intensify the force of the utterance, which (we need to remember) is a rebuke for human presumption toward God. Repetition is a second rhetorical device on display in the passage. For example, the selection is a virtual showcase of syntactic parallelism in which the second line of a two-line

previous: Eugène Isabe, *A Storm off the Normandy Coast*, probably 1850s

unit parallels the thought and grammatical structure of the first line using different words and images. And then, as an added layer, the poem repeatedly uses the same opening formula in successive units. For example, six times the poet begins a question with the formula, "Have you . . . ?" Seven times he asks, "Who . . . ?" And so forth.

As we ponder the individual questions and figurative descriptions of nature, we will have our picture of both God and nature expanded. And since the medium of all the sublimity is imagination, poetry, and rhetoric, our admiration for these gifts from God can also be amplified. ■

Literary portrayals of the sublime in nature achieve their effect partly through focusing on the large agents of nature. Psalm 95:4–5 illustrates this, in microcosm, the same way our selection from Job does on a huge scale:

> In his hand are the depths of the earth;
> > the heights of the mountains are his also.
> The sea is his, for he made it,
> > and his hands formed the dry land.

Job, 1618/30—the Latin inscription says, "NOLI ME CONDEMNARE" ("do not condemn me")

The Archetypal River
Medley

Ezekiel 47:6–9

THEN [THE LORD God] led me back to the bank of the river. As I went back, I saw on the bank of the river very many trees on the one side and on the other. And he said to me, . . . "Everything will live where the river goes."

William Wordsworth (1770–1850)

O glide, fair stream! forever so,
Thy quiet soul on all bestowing,
Till all our minds forever flow
As thy deep waters now are flowing.

Charles Dickens (1812–1870)

IT WAS PLEASANT AND QUIET out there with the sails on the river passing beyond the earthwork, and sometimes, when the tide was low, looking as they belong to sunken ships that were still sailing on at the bottom of the water. . . . As I watched the vessels standing, the light struck aslant, afar off, upon a cloud or sail or green hillside or water line.

Kenneth Grahame (1859–1932)

He thought his happiness was complete when, as he meandered aimlessly along, suddenly he stood by the edge of a full-fed river. Never in his life had he seen a river before this sleek, sinuous, full-bodied animal, chasing and chuckling, gripping things with a gurgle and leaving them with a laugh, to fling itself on fresh playmates that shook themselves free, and were caught and held again. All was a-shake and a-shivver—glints and gleams and sparkles, rustle and swirl, chatter and bubble. . . . He sat on the bank, while the river still chattered on to him, a babbling procession of the best stories in the world, sent from the heart of the earth to be told at last to the insatiable sea.

Spiritual

I've got peace like a river,
I've got peace like a river,
I've got peace like a river in my soul.

Frances Havergal (1836–1879)

Like a river glorious
Is God's perfect peace,
Over all victorious
In its bright increase;
Perfect, yet it floweth
Fuller every day;
Perfect, yet it groweth
Deeper all the way.

The Archetypal River

THE PURPOSE OF THIS ENTRY IS THREEFOLD. The first is to codify our own experiences of rivers, reminding us of our feelings toward them and sharpening our understanding of the meaning of a river in human experience. The second is to further our love of nature writing by demonstrating the range of literary genres that touch on nature. The third is to expand our spiritual understanding by exploring how nature provides a repository of spiritual symbols.

The key to all three of these is the archetype. Archetypes are the recurrent images and motifs that we encounter throughout life and in literature. They make up the groundwork of human experience. The river is one such archetype: a Christian author has suggested in his memoir that "it's likely that a river flows through every life of every American in every generation." Yet so are virtually all the other nature images that appear in this anthology. The garden or park is an archetype, for example. Sunrise and sunset are archetypes. So are the seasons.

A good starting point for analyzing an archetype is therefore to think about our own experiences with one in particular—such as, in this case, the river. What goes on inside us as we cross a river or stand beside it? The passages of this entry demonstrate the possible meanings of the archetypal river as explored by the artistic imagination in literature. The smooth-flowing river is an image of peacefulness, first of all. Then, as we move from the aesthetic realm to the utilitarian, we recognize that rivers are lifegiving—not only for the creatures that live in them but also to animals, plants, and people on land.

The familiar hymn by Frances Havergal can serve as a short course for us on assimilating nature as a spiritual symbol. The wrong way to handle "Like a River Glorious" would be to dismiss its river simile and lavish all our attention on what it ultimately says about God's peace being perfect, victorious, and bright, as well as always increasing. The author wanted readers to unpack the literal meanings of a river before carrying them over to the spiritual life. When we do so, we see rivers in a new way. They are *glorious*. They fill us with *peace*. They are *victorious*, in the sense that they engulf and cover any object in their path. They are *perfect* or complete, and yet they are prone to increasing and growing *fuller* and *deeper all the way*. ∎

Frits Thaulow, *Picquigny*, 1899

The Archetypal River

There are many evocative river passages in the Bible. Psalm 46:4 is a worthy representative. After the opening verses of this psalm have pictured destructive earthquakes and tsunamis and roaring waters, the imagery is reversed by a single announcement: "There is a river whose streams make glad."

Lessons from Nature

CHARLES SPURGEON (1834–1892)

SOME IN THESE modern times have thought it to be a mark of high spirituality never to observe nature. I remember sorrowfully reading... of a godly person who, in sailing down one of the most famous rivers in the world, closed his eyes, lest the picturesque beauties of the scene should divert his mind from scriptural topics. This may be regarded by some as profound spirituality; to me it seems to savor of absurdity. There may be persons who think they have grown in grace when they have attained to this; it seems to me that they are growing out of their senses. To despise the creating work of God—what is it but... to despise God himself?... To despise the Maker is a sin; to think little of God as the Creator is a crime.

We ourselves would not think it an honor to us if our friends considered our productions to be unworthy of admiration, and injurious to their minds.... If when they passed our workmanship they turned their eyes away, lest they should suffer injury by looking at it, we should not regard them as respectful to us. Surely the despising of that which is made is akin to the despising of the Maker himself. David tells us that "the Lord shall rejoice in his works." If he rejoices in what he has made, shall not those who have communion with him rejoice in his works also?

"The works of the Lord are great, sought out of them that have pleasure therein." Despise not the work, lest you despise the worker. . . .

The birds of the air, and the fish of the sea, the glorious sunrise and sunset, the snow-clad Alps, the ancient forests, the mysterious glaciers, the boundless ocean [must not be disparaged]. . . . Here on this earth is Calvary where the Savior died, and by his sacrifice . . . he made this outer world a temple wherein everything doth speak of God's glory. . . . This world is but a nether heaven; it is but the lower chamber of which the upper story glows with the full splendor of God, where angels see him face to face, and this lower story is not without glory. . . .

Rest assured that he who wrote the Bible, the second and clearest revelation of his divine mind, wrote also the first book, the book of nature; and who are we that we should derogate from the worth of the first because we esteem the second. . . . There is no quarrel between nature and revelation. . . . The one illustrates and establishes the other. Walking in the fields at eventide, as Isaac did, I see in the ripening harvest the same God of whom I read in the word that he covenanted that seed-time and harvest should not cease. Surveying the midnight skies, I remember him who, while he calls the stars by their names, also binds up the broken in heart. [Some choose to] neglect the volume of creation, or the volume of revelation; I shall delight in them both as long as I live. ∎

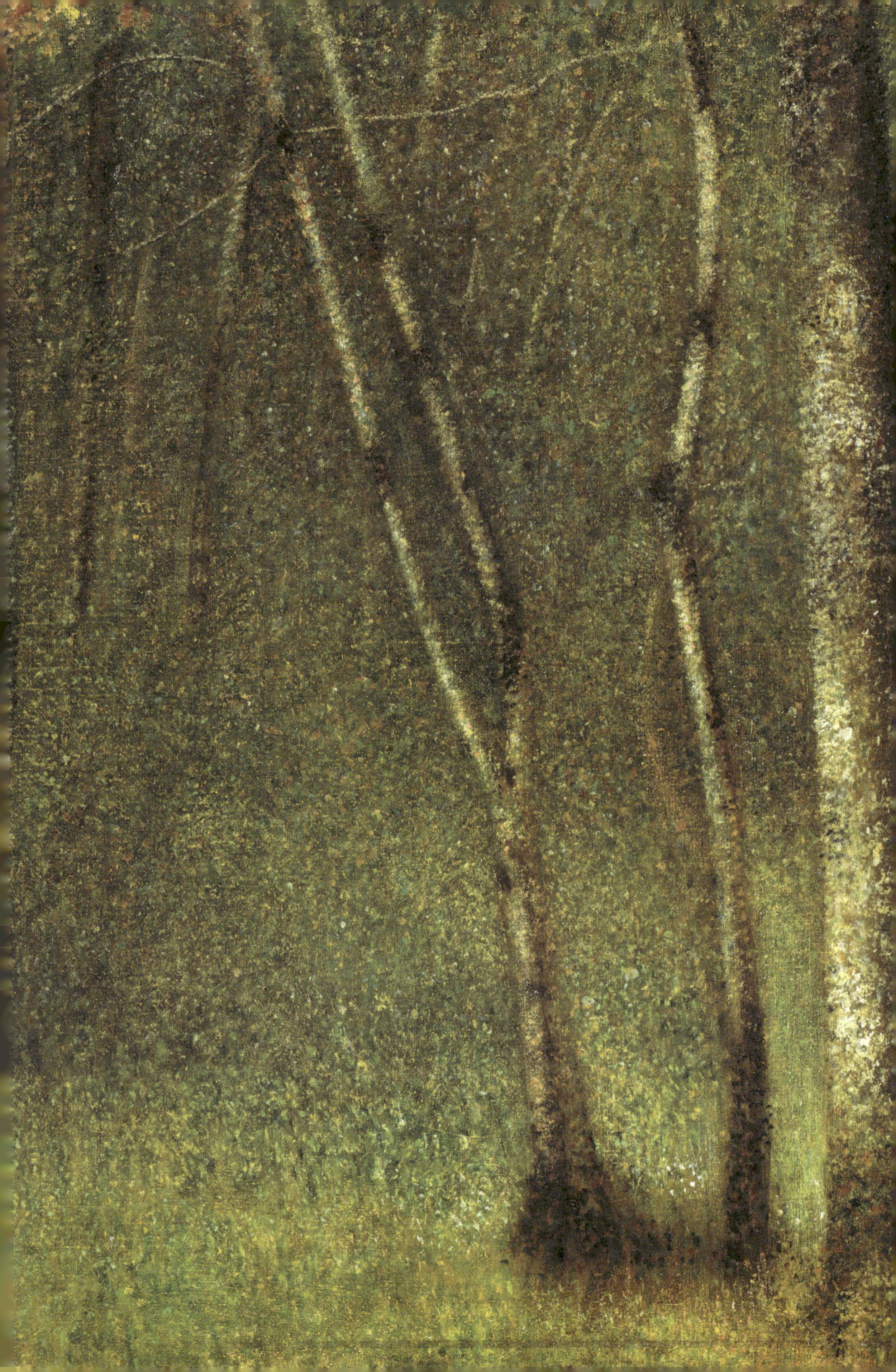

Lessons from Nature

O NE OF THE BEST-KEPT SECRETS relating to the famous Victorian preacher Charles Spurgeon is his book *Teachings of Nature in the Kingdom of Grace*. Published after his death, it is a collection of his sermons on virtually all the important nature texts in the Bible, from Genesis 1 to Revelation 22. It may be treated as a systematic guide to nature writing within the Bible. While its sermons offer continuous glimpses of Spurgeon's love of nature, they also belong to a longstanding Christian tradition that treats the agents of nature as analogues or symbols of the spiritual life. The sermons' focus thus necessarily falls on the spiritual half of the equation rather than on physical nature. The specific sermon from which this passage is taken shows us more about Spurgeon's views on nature itself.

Spurgeon writes as an observer of nature who takes time to incorporate meditation on nature into his daily life. This may seem unlikely. Spurgeon was the preacher at a church with over five thousand members. This church was in the heart of London—which, at the time, was the world's largest city. Spurgeon himself was a bookish man—one who even took time to found a college for ministers. Therefore, we should read this passage with an awareness that if Spurgeon could find time to contemplate nature, so can we.

This passage is the introduction to a sermon that explores how God provides for life on our planet, and especially animal life, through nature. The genre of these opening remarks is polemical, conducting an argument. In fact, we can read this passage as Spurgeon's half of a debate. His opponents are Christians who, while on a pursuit of what they regard to be more spiritual matters, consider nature unworthy of attention. What was true then is true now as well: nature is a neglected subject within the evangelical church. Most readers of this anthology likely cannot recall hearing a sermon that has explained and espoused a well-thought-out Christian view of nature.

This neglect is why it is important for us to heed the logic of Spurgeon's defense of nature. His first argument on nature's behalf is that disparaging it means belittling the God who created and sustains it. To buttress this idea, Spurgeon draws a parallel to how we feel when something we have made is ignored by an acquaintance. A second argument is an appeal to scriptural authority—and specifically the assertions in the Bible that nature is important to God and to its writers such as, and particularly,

Georges Seurat, *The Forest at Pontaubert*, 1881

the psalmists. Third, Spurgeon claims that Christ's incarnation, and his redemptive life on earth, have consecrated our physical world and given it supreme worth. Throughout this passage, Spurgeon uses forceful metaphors, comparing nature to a *temple wherein everything doth speak of God's glory* and to the *first book* that God wrote.

We start to make this passage our own by considering the intellectual and doctrinal principles of its argument, then by being attentive to nature as we experience it. Guided by Spurgeon's concluding paragraph, we may also bring passages from the Bible to mind as we encounter nature in our daily lives. ■

The passage on which Spurgeon preached the full version of his five-point sermon was Psalm 104:17–18:

> In them the birds build their nests;
> > the stork has her home in the fir trees.
> The high mountains are for the wild goats;
> > the rocks are a refuge for the rock badgers.

Sam Ferrara, *Matterhorn Sunset*, 2016

Communing with God through Nature

GEORGE WASHINGTON CARVER (CA. 1864–1943)

As soon as you begin to read the great and loving God out of all forms of existence He has created, both animate and inanimate, then you will be able to converse with Him, anywhere, everywhere, and at all times. Oh, what a fullness of joy will come to you.... God is speaking....

I ask the Great Creator silently daily, and often many times per day, to permit me to speak to Him through the three great Kingdoms of the world, which He has created, viz.—the animal, mineral and vegetable Kingdoms; their relations to each other, to us, our relations to them and the Great God who made all of us....

We get closer to God as we get more intimately and understandingly acquainted with the things he has created.... More and more as we come closer and closer in touch with nature and its teachings are we able to see the Divine and are therefore fitted to interpret correctly the various languages spoken by all forms of nature about us....

First, ... nature in its varied forms are the little windows through which God permits me to commune with Him, and to see much of His glory, majesty, and power by simply lifting the curtain and looking in.

Second, I love to think of nature as unlimited broadcasting stations, through which God speaks to us every day, every hour and every moment of our lives, if we will only tune in and remain so.

Third, I am more and more convinced, as I search for truth, that no student of nature can "Behold the lilies of the field," or "Look unto the hills," or study even the microscopic wonders of a stagnant pool of water, and honestly declare himself to be an Infidel....

To those who have as yet not learned the secret of true happiness, which is the joy of coming into the closest relationship with the Maker and Preserver of all things: begin now to study the little things in your own door yard, going from the known to the nearest related unknown, for indeed each new truth brings one nearer to God. ∎

On a first reading, Carver's enthusiasm for nature's ability to be a channel for us to commune with God may seem overstated, but Carver earned both the spiritual and the scientific right to say what he does.

What Carver called his "simple conversion" occurred at the age of ten. His account of it is as follows: "God just came into my heart one afternoon while I was alone in the 'loft' of our big barn while I was shelling corn. . . . [I] knelt down by the barrel of corn and prayed as best I could." As an adult, Carver had a long ministry to others, especially young people. By profession, Carver was a research scientist and one of the most famous agronomists in American history. His specialty became the peanut plant. Thus, if we combine the spiritual sensitivity of Carver with his scientific expertise in plants, his comments about communing with God through nature fall into place.

For centuries of religious contemplation, especially in the monastic tradition, practitioners have championed the creation of set-apart places of natural beauty, such as enclosed gardens, in which the righteous may offer up their thoughts and prayers to God. Carver's claim is quite the opposite. The nature of which he speaks is not set apart and enclosed; rather, he speaks of all the places that he visits during his daily routine as a botanist—and that we visit in *our* daily routines. Additionally, the passage is oriented not toward our prayers ascending to God but rather toward revelations of truth descending from God to us. Carver's soul is devoted not to talking to God but instead to listening with an awareness that *God is speaking*.

To convey these ideas, Carver gravitated to metaphors as his medium. Thus the forms of nature are little windows through which we see *much* of God's *glory, majesty, and power*. Nature's details are broadcasting stations through which God speaks.

Carver's primary interest is not the philosophical or theological principle that nature reveals God. Rather, using that principle as the foundation, he focuses on relating to God and communing with him through devotion. Every paragraph of the passage expresses a desire for nature to lead us to relate more intimately to God. Carver sees nature not as an end in itself but as a means of bringing us *nearer to God*. Even as he raises the bar high, he speaks with the voice of a compassionate teacher, encouraging us in his concluding paragraph to begin by studying the *little things in [our] own door yard*.

Communing with God through Nature

This passage offers two things for us to take away: we can resolve to practice Carver's program of seeing and hearing God everywhere within nature and can then go on to *converse* and *commune* with God. ∎

This entire passage is rooted in a truth expressed in Romans 1:20, that God's "eternal power and divine nature . . . have been clearly perceived, ever since the creation of the world, in the things that have been made."

Anton Dieffenbach, *Window*, 1856

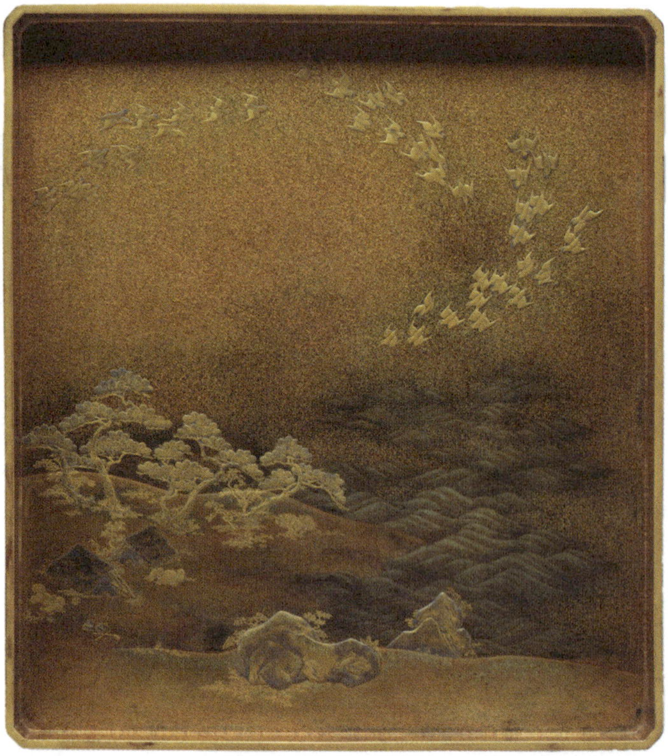

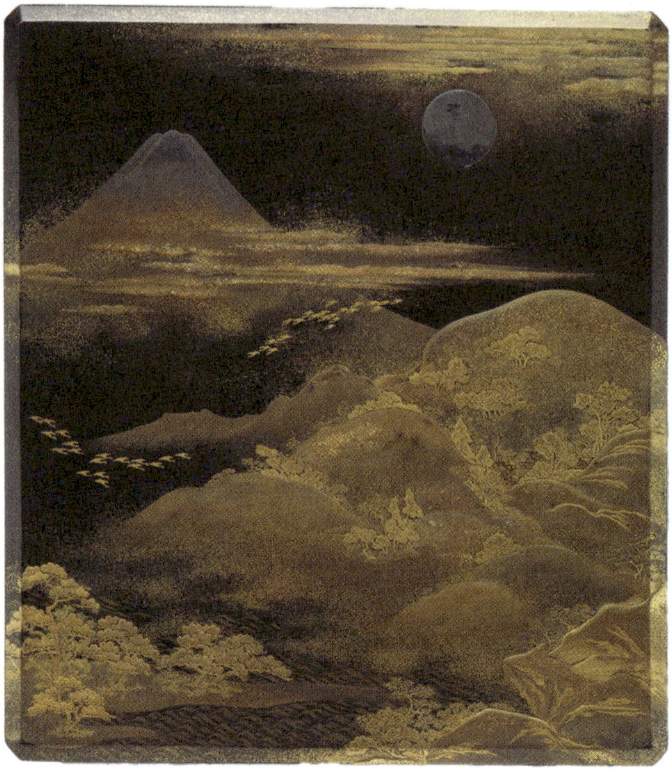

God's Grandeur
Gerard Manley Hopkins (1844–1889)

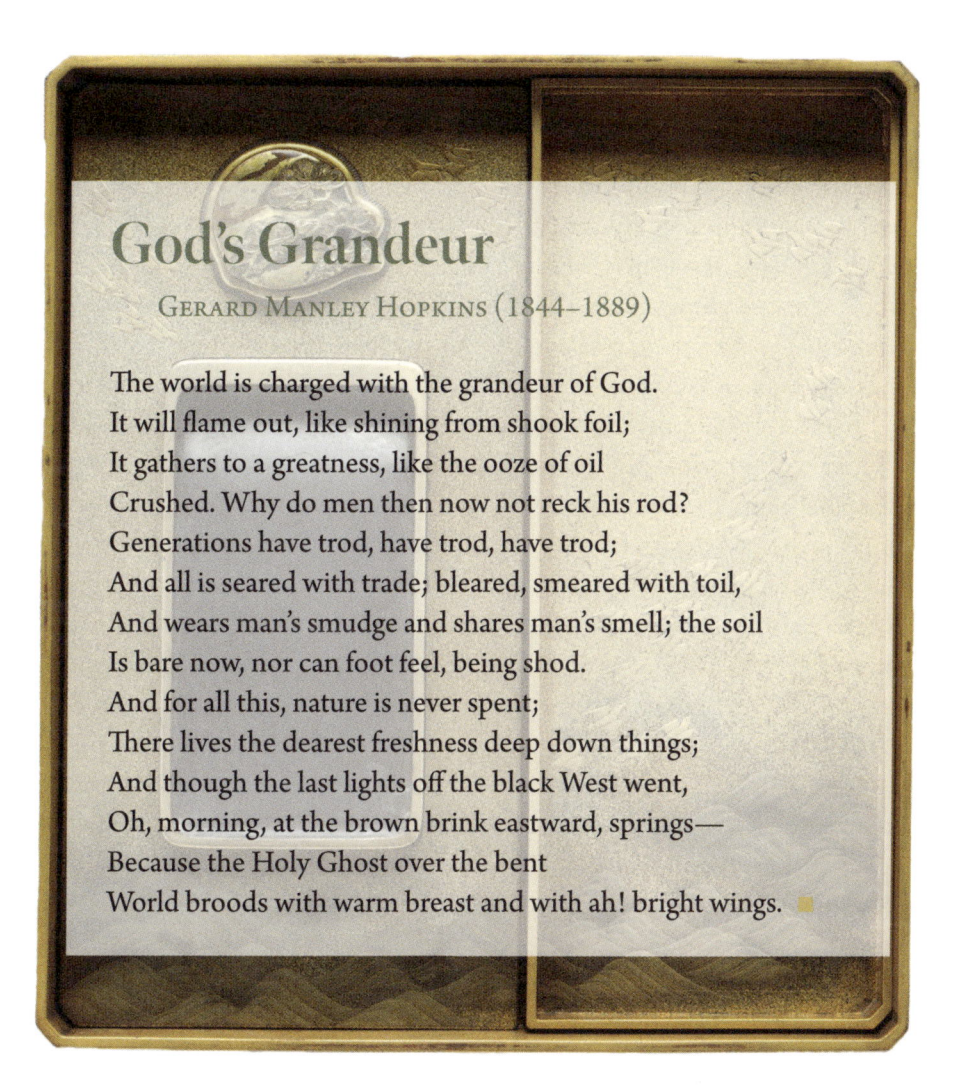

The world is charged with the grandeur of God.
It will flame out, like shining from shook foil;
It gathers to a greatness, like the ooze of oil
Crushed. Why do men then now not reck his rod?
Generations have trod, have trod, have trod;
And all is seared with trade; bleared, smeared with toil,
And wears man's smudge and shares man's smell; the soil
Is bare now, nor can foot feel, being shod.
And for all this, nature is never spent;
There lives the dearest freshness deep down things;
And though the last lights off the black West went,
Oh, morning, at the brown brink eastward, springs—
Because the Holy Ghost over the bent
World broods with warm breast and with ah! bright wings.

God's Grandeur

As we unpack the opening line of this sonnet, we can see that it announces what the entire remainder of the poem will elaborate. By *world* Hopkins means the world of nature. The verb *charged* encompasses three simultaneous actions: (1) God's grandeur energizes nature, (2) God gives nature the task or responsibility of exhibiting his grandeur, and (3) nature forcefully thrusts this entrusted message forward, like a charging army. The word *grandeur* conveys the meaning of artistic splendor, and it overcomes the cliché effect that has settled on the word *greatness*. Finally, the opening line ascribes nature's grandeur to God, which makes it a praise psalm.

The rest of the poem presents variations on the theme that has been announced. Some of nature's grandeur is overwhelming and eye-catching, like light glinting off metallic foil. Other effects of nature only gradually impress themselves on us, the way oil is crushed from olives and other plants. Because Hopkins writes in the tradition of nineteenth-century Romanticism, he cannot look at the grandeur of nature without contrasting it to the way in which the human race has exploited, ransacked, and depleted nature, so he devotes five lines to lamenting the effects of civilization.

But then, in a surprise move, Hopkins optimistically asserts that humankind hasn't ruined nature after all. God replenishes nature in such a way that it is perpetually fresh, the poet maintains, before ending with a four-line example: the darkness of night is always and predictably followed by sunrise.

The view that nature is infused with God's presence, which this poem takes to a notable degree, is called a sacramental view of nature. Hopkins clinches this view by ascribing the perpetual re-creation of nature to the Holy Spirit—in reference to the description in Genesis 1:2 of how "the Spirit of God was hovering [or brooding] over the face of the waters."

As we assimilate this poem, we can resolve to be good stewards of nature rather than the kind of poor stewards that Hopkins describes, and we can celebrate the presence of God's grandeur in nature. ■

Box for inkstone and writing implements (Japan), early to mid-1800s

God's Grandeur

A sacramental view of nature subtly appears in the poem's accusation that modern people cannot feel the soil because their feet are *shod* with shoes. This is not a naive Romantic invitation to go barefoot but instead an allusion to the story of Moses and the burning bush: "Then [God] said, . . . 'Take your sandals off your feet, for the place on which you are standing is holy ground'" (Ex. 3:5). The stance of Hopkins's poem is that all of nature is holy ground.

Dierick Bouts the Elder, *Moses and the Burning Bush, with Moses Removing His Shoes*, ca. 1465–70

These All Look to You

PSALM 104

Bless the Lord, O my soul!
    O Lord my God, you are very great!
You are clothed with splendor and majesty,
    covering yourself with light as with a garment,
    stretching out the heavens like a tent.
He lays the beams of his chambers on the waters;
he makes the clouds his chariot;
    he rides on the wings of the wind;
he makes his messengers winds,
    his ministers a flaming fire.

He set the earth on its foundations,
    so that it should never be moved.
You covered it with the deep as with a garment;
    the waters stood above the mountains.
At your rebuke they fled;
    at the sound of your thunder they took to flight.
The mountains rose, the valleys sank down
    to the place that you appointed for them.
You set a boundary that they may not pass,
    so that they might not again cover the earth.

You make springs gush forth in the valleys;
    they flow between the hills;
they give drink to every beast of the field;
    the wild donkeys quench their thirst.
Beside them the birds of the heavens dwell;
    they sing among the branches.
From your lofty abode you water the mountains;
    the earth is satisfied with the fruit of your work.

You cause the grass to grow for the livestock
    and plants for man to cultivate,
that he may bring forth food from the earth
    and wine to gladden the heart of man,
oil to make his face shine
    and bread to strengthen man's heart.

The trees of the Lord are watered abundantly,
    the cedars of Lebanon that he planted.
In them the birds build their nests;
    the stork has her home in the fir trees.
The high mountains are for the wild goats;
    the rocks are a refuge for the rock badgers.

These All Look to You

He made the moon to mark the seasons;
    the sun knows its time for setting.
You make darkness, and it is night,
    when all the beasts of the forest creep about.
The young lions roar for their prey,
    seeking their food from God.
When the sun rises, they steal away
    and lie down in their dens.
Man goes out to his work
    and to his labor until the evening.

O Lord, how manifold are your works!
    In wisdom have you made them all;
    the earth is full of your creatures.
Here is the sea, great and wide,
    which teems with creatures innumerable,
    living things both small and great.
There go the ships,
    and Leviathan, which you formed to play in it.

previous (left): Shrimp (Moche), 500–600s; Goat (Mycenaean), 1300s BC; Camelid (Inca), 1400–1535; Animal pendant (Central America), ca. 1–1000; Hawk (Assyrian), ca. 1700s BC; Lion (German), ca. 1732; Tuning key (North China), 200s BC; Textile ornament (Chimú), 1300–1400s; Writing box (Japan), 1600s

These All Look to You

These all look to you,
    to give them their food in due season.
When you give it to them, they gather it up;
    when you open your hand, they are filled with good things.
When you hide your face, they are dismayed;
    when you take away their breath, they die
    and return to their dust.
When you send forth your Spirit, they are created,
    and you renew the face of the ground.

May the glory of the Lord endure forever;
    may the Lord rejoice in his works,
who looks on the earth and it trembles,
    who touches the mountains and they smoke!
I will sing to the Lord as long as I live;
    I will sing praise to my God while I have being.
May my meditation be pleasing to him,
    for I rejoice in the Lord.
Let sinners be consumed from the earth,
    and let the wicked be no more!
Bless the Lord O my soul!
Praise the Lord! ∎

previous (right): Birdstone (Archaic), 1500–500 BC; Bull (Hittite), ca. 1300–1200s BC; Toad (Italy), possibly 1500s; Leaf bead (New Kingdom), ca. 1390–1352 BC; Terracotta vessel (Cypriot), 1900–1600 BC; Animal figurine (Middle Kingdom), ca. 1981–1640 BC; Cat (Middle Kingdom), ca. 1990–1900 BC

These All Look to You

Here is the most exalted nature poem in the Psalter. Only the genre known as the ode could sustain the grandeur of such a composition. A long and complex lyric poem written in a high style, an ode does justice to the dignity of the subject it celebrates. This psalm runs true to form.

Part of the grandeur of an ode comes from what literary scholars call its *architectonics*—its structure or organization. The arrangement of the content of Psalm 104 is an artistic feat in itself. The poem progresses as follows: stanza 1 introduces the function of nature (to serve God); stanza 2 considers the origin of nature (how it was created by God); stanzas 3 through 7 look at the ways nature (arranged according to earth, sky, and sea) provides for its inhabitants; stanza 8 summarizes the behavior of all these inhabitants, beginning with a statement that *these all look to you*; and the final stanza unleashes an explosion of lyric responses to the God of nature.

The poem's survey of nature covers all the bases, but an ode is characterized by unity as well as amplitude—it must show a control and focus commensurate with its abundance. Thus, the first two lines of its final stanza highlight the unifying core of this particular ode: the declaration that nature displays the perpetual *glory of the Lord* and that God *rejoice[s] in his works*—in a way reminiscent of the statement that God "saw everything that he had made, and behold, it was very good" (Gen. 1:31).

Once we have grasped the overall design and content of this psalm, we can enjoy unpacking the wealth of figurative description of nature that it puts on display. For example, the sky above is a metaphoric tent. The solid land next to a lake or sea is like the foundation of a house. The fast-moving clouds are a chariot. Then, when we reach the extended middle section that the poem devotes to God's provision for the creatures of earth, its figurative mode gives way to an album of snapshots of nature that it describes more directly (such as the way that the birds *sing among the branches* of trees).

All these poetic techniques provide a wonderful occasion for us to contemplate how expansive nature is, as we consider how many creatures God cares for day by day, and additionally how magnificent he is to have created the universe and to continue to provide for it. ■

Psalm 104 surveys the nature of the earth, sky, and sea, and, throughout it, the poet ascribes glory to God for his creation and provision of this expansive realm. Isaiah 6:3 puts all this into kernel form when it states that "the whole earth is full of his glory."

The House That God Built and Furnished

Martin Luther (1483–1546)
and Caedmon (ca. 657–684)

Commentary on Genesis, 1500s

After God adorned the roof of man's home, the sky, and added the light, he spread its floor and made the earth a suitable place for people to live.... Beautifully did God form ... the foundation and roof of this house.... Its foundation is the earth. Its walls are the mighty waters on every side. God next made provision for our food. He commanded the earth to bring forth herbs and trees to bear fruit of every kind....

We should consider the divine care and goodness exercised on our behalf, in that God prepared such a beautiful dwelling for Adam ... before he created him, so that when he was created, he might find a home already prepared and furnished. Into this home, ready and furnished, God led him ... and commanded him to enjoy all the fruits and provisions of his ample abode.

On the third day God prepared the food and a pantry in which to store it. On the fourth day the sun and the moon were given for the service of man. On the fifth day rule was committed to him over the fishes and the birds. On the sixth day the same rule was entrusted to him over all the beasts, that he might use all the rich blessings of these creatures freely, according to his necessities. As a return, God only required that man should acknowledge the goodness of his Creator and live in his fear and worship. This peculiar care of God over us and for us even before we were created may be contemplated ... with great benefit to our souls.

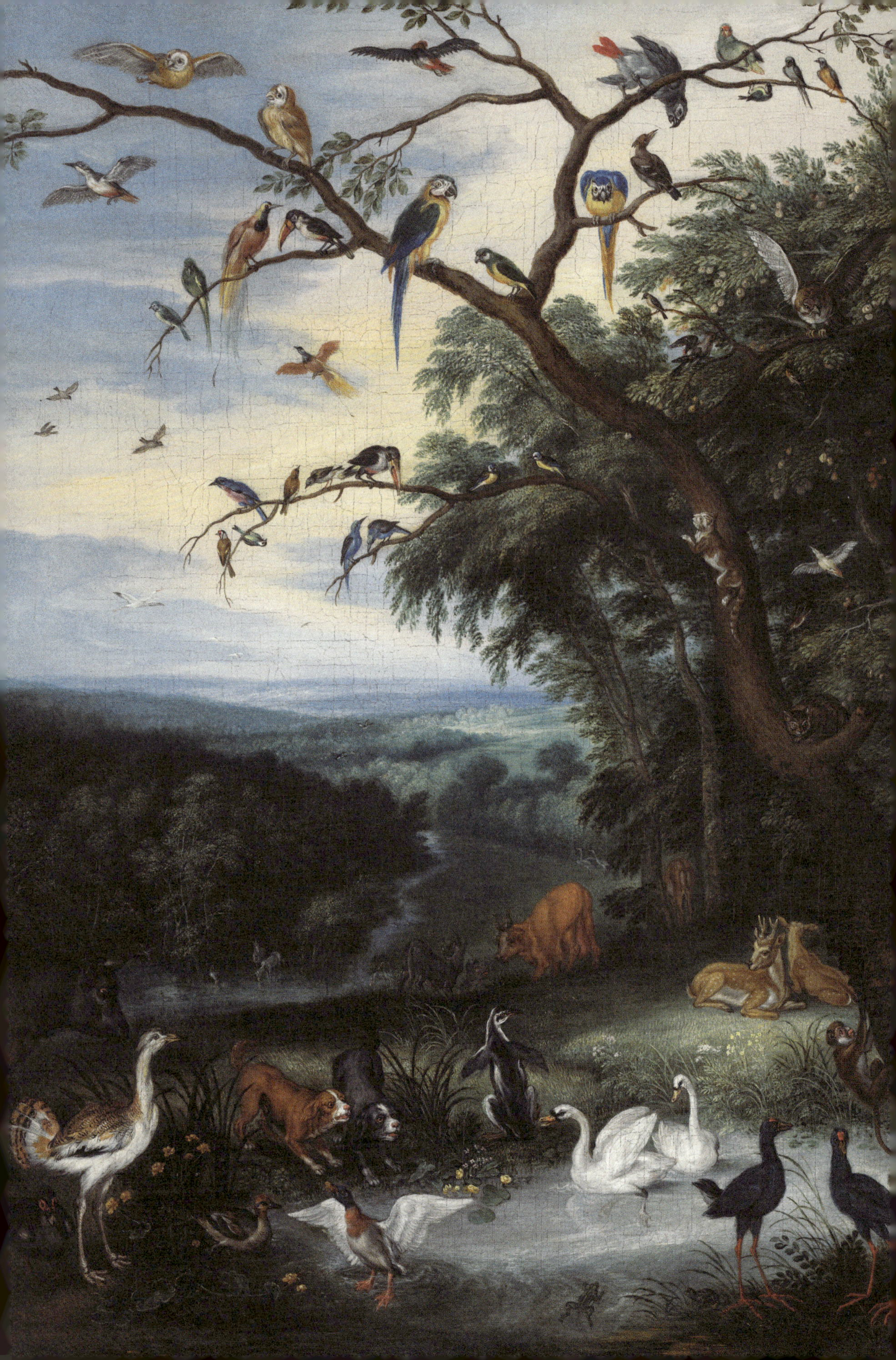

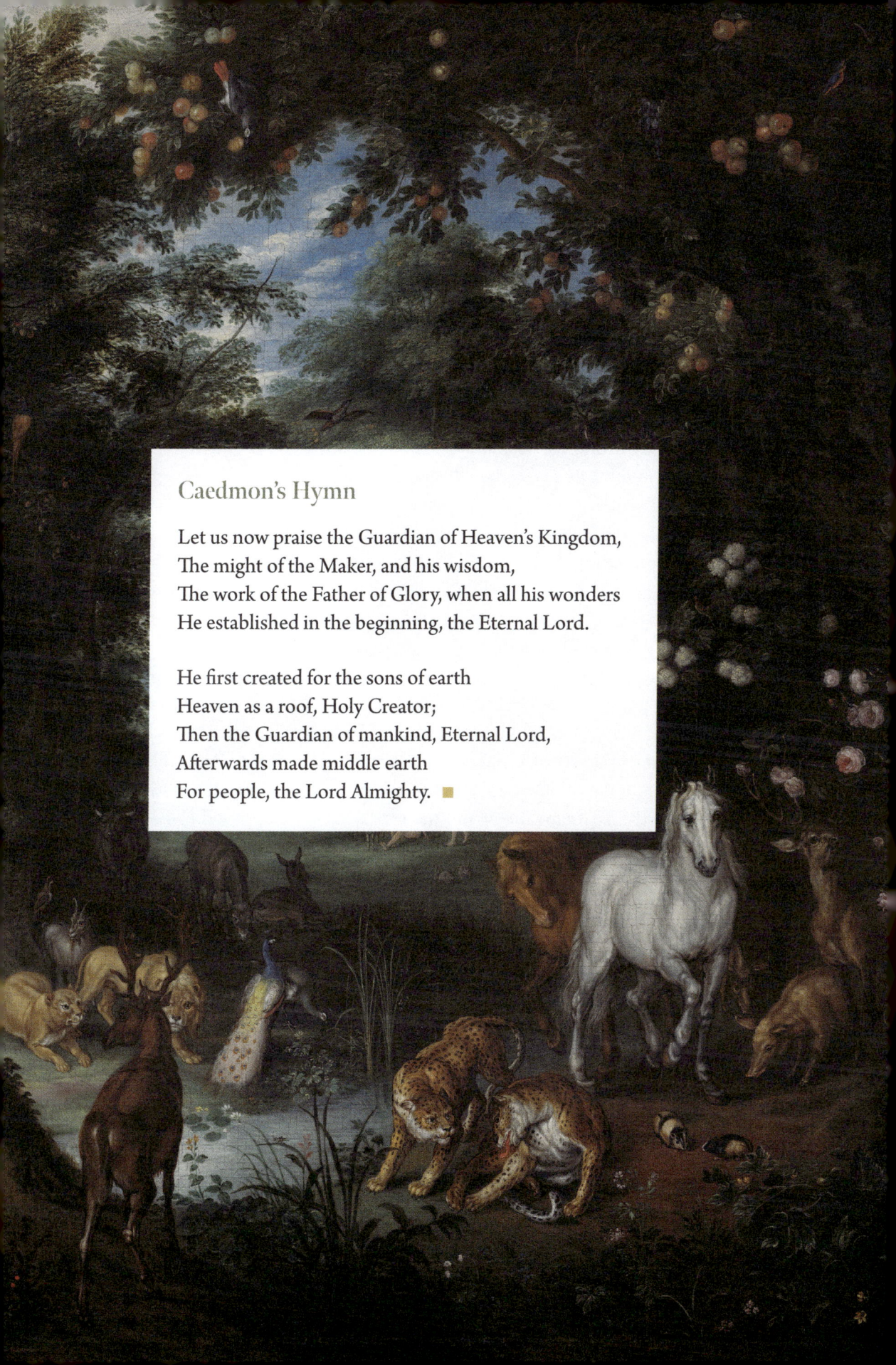

Caedmon's Hymn

Let us now praise the Guardian of Heaven's Kingdom,
The might of the Maker, and his wisdom,
The work of the Father of Glory, when all his wonders
He established in the beginning, the Eternal Lord.

He first created for the sons of earth
Heaven as a roof, Holy Creator;
Then the Guardian of mankind, Eternal Lord,
Afterwards made middle earth
For people, the Lord Almighty. ∎

A PRELIMINARY WORD NEEDS TO BE said about the importance of Caedmon's poem and the famous story of its origin. Composed in Old English, it is the oldest surviving work of English literature. The author was an illiterate farmhand who worked at Whitby Abbey in northeast England. After mealtimes, it was a practice for the abbey's residents to take turns singing a song to entertain the others. As the harp was passed from one singer to the next, Caedmon often found an excuse to leave the dining hall before it reached him. On one of these occasions, he went to the barn and fell asleep. In a dream, he heard someone commanding him to sing. When he replied that he did not know how to sing, the speaker replied, "Sing about creation." Thereupon Caedmon composed the poem known as "Caedmon's Hymn."

The two texts that comprise this entry fill an important niche in this anthology of nature writing. The point of departure for both Luther and Caedmon is the creation story told in Genesis 1. It is important for us not to overlook the fact that Genesis 1 is nature writing. From start to finish, it situates us in the world of nature. Like the biblical account, Luther and Caedmon highlight the Creator of nature, but their writing then proceeds to move in a fresh direction.

Luther and Caedmon develop the idea that the created world is a home that God built for the human race. They convey this partly through such architectural vocabulary as *roof, foundation, house,* and *pantry*. This architectural metaphor is not as evident in Caedmon's hymn as it is in Luther's exposition of the creation story, but it is still present through the hymn's motifs of the sky being a *roof* and the world being an enclosed place of safety (*middle earth*), as well as through its emphasis on God's provision of nature being specifically for the *sons of earth* and for *people*.

Caedmon's poem is more obviously literary than Luther's commentary. It is a psalm of praise modeled on the Old Testament examples of that genre. Its first stanza is a call to praise, and its second stanza conducts this praise by cataloging God's mighty acts of creation. It further exalts God with a string of epithets, or titles: *Guardian of Heaven's Kingdom, Father of Glory, Eternal Lord, Holy Creator*.

Upon a closer look, however, Luther's commentary shows itself to be equally literary, as can be seen in the way that he builds his message around the central metaphor of nature being a *home*. We associate home with such qualities as safety, comfort, protection, provision, eating, resting, and

Izaak van Oosten, *The Garden of Eden*, between 1655 and 1661

beauty. Luther does not spell out all these qualities, but he equips us to do so ourselves by giving us this metaphor as a springboard for our thinking about nature.

The best way to appropriate what this entry offers is to analyze its metaphor of nature as a home that God designed and built for us. We start by codifying what the concept of home means to us personally. How might it affect our experience of nature to see these qualities in it? ∎

The text from which spring our two readings in this entry is the Bible's creation story, whose famous opening sentence is a theme statement for what follows: "In the beginning, God created the heavens and the earth" (Gen. 1:1).

Charles Sheeler, *Home, Sweet Home*, 1931

A Prayer in Spring

ROBERT FROST (1874–1963)

Oh, give us pleasure in the flowers today;
And give us not to think so far away
As the uncertain harvest; keep us here
All simply in the springing of the year.

Oh, give us pleasure in the orchard white,
Like nothing else by day, like ghosts by night;
And make us happy in the happy bees,
The swarm dilating round the perfect trees.

And make us happy in the darting bird
That suddenly above the bees is heard,
The meteor that thrusts in with needle bill,
And off a blossom in mid air stands still.

For this is love and nothing else is love,
To which it is reserved for God above
To sanctify to what far ends he will,
But which it only needs that we fulfill.

THE TITLE OF THIS POEM tells us all we need to know to navigate it: that the genre of the poem is, first of all, a prayer. We will go on to realize that it is, moreover, a communal prayer—as many of the psalms and our own public prayers are. It is, more specifically, a petitionary prayer, which prompts us to follow its speaker's lead by asking God to enable us to experience spring in the best possible way and without allowing anything to distract us.

Before we analyze what this "best way" is, we should note the second half of the poem's title, which alerts us to another genre that it occupies. This is the genre of the *reverdi*—a poem that celebrates the coming of spring. Most major English and American poets have written one or more of these. The main strategy of a reverdi is to catalog the sensory pleasures of spring, leading us to vicariously experience them. As we read Frost's poem, we feel that we are taking a walk in an orchard. Its second stanza focuses on the white blossoms of trees, which by day appear as they really are—*like nothing else*—and by night as indistinct white ghosts. That stanza also paints a picture of swarming, *happy* bees. The third stanza devotes its attention to a hummingbird that flashes into sight like a meteor, thrusts its thin beak (its *needle bill*) into a blossom, and then hovers stationary in the air.

The poem is a prayer for enablement, and as we look closely at the speaker's petitions, we see that its primary petition is that God will enable

Martin Johnson Heade, *Hummingbird and Apple Blossoms*, 1875 us to revel in the pleasures of the spring season, undisturbed by distractions. The poem's opening stanza admits the distraction that tempts us to leap forward from the present springtime moment to a worry about whether there will be an adequate harvest at the end of summer—a farmer's viewpoint, to be sure. The potential distraction in the last stanza is to think we need to know the ultimate mysteries that only God knows. Here the poet breaks from his petitionary prayer to admonish his fellow humans. Loving the spring season needs to suffice; we summon the faith to believe that God will sanctify our love of nature in springtime as he fulfills his purposes for us. ▪

The central thrust of Frost's poem is encapsulated in Psalm 118:24: "This is the day that the Lord has made; let us rejoice and be glad in it."

George Inness, *Spring Blossoms, Montclair, New Jersey*, ca. 1891

Like a Bridegroom Leaving His Chamber

King David and Mark Twain (1835–1910)

Psalm 19:1–6

The heavens declare the glory of God,
    and the sky above proclaims his handiwork.
Day to day pours out speech,
    and night to night reveals knowledge.
There is no speech, nor are there words,
    whose voice is not heard.
Their voice goes out through all the earth,
    and their words to the end of the world.

In them he has set a tent for the sun,
    which comes out like a bridegroom leaving his chamber,
    and, like a strong man, runs its course with joy.
Its rising is from the end of the heavens,
    and its circuit to the end of them,
    and there is nothing hidden from its heat.

Life on the Mississippi, 1883

ONE CANNOT SEE too many summer sunrises on the Mississippi. They are enchanting. First, there is the eloquence of silence; for a deep hush broods everywhere. Next, there is the haunting sense of loneliness, isolation, remoteness from the worry and bustle of the world. The dawn creeps in stealthily; the solid walls of black forest soften to gray, and vast stretches of the river open up and reveal themselves; the water is glass-smooth, gives off spectral little wreaths of white mist, there is not the faintest breath of wind, nor stir of leaf; the tranquility is profound and infinitely satisfying.

Then a bird pipes up, another follows, and soon the pipings develop into a jubilant riot of music. You see none of the birds; you simply move through an atmosphere of song which seems to sing itself. When the light has become a little stronger, you have one of the fairest and softest pictures imaginable. You have the intense green of the massed and crowded foliage near by; you see it paling shade by shade in front of you; upon the next projecting cape, a mile off or more, the tint has lightened to the tender young green of spring; the cape beyond that one has almost lost color, and the furthest one, miles away under the horizon, sleeps upon the water a mere dim vapor, and hardly separable from the sky above it and about it. And all this stretch of river is a mirror, and you have the shadowy reflections of the leafage and the curving shores and the receding capes pictured in it.

Well, that is all beautiful; soft and rich and beautiful; and when the sun gets well up, and distributes a pink flush here and a powder of gold yonder and a purple haze where it will yield the best effect, you grant that you have seen something that is worth remembering. ■

I**N THESE TWO DESCRIPTIONS OF** the sun, we find a unified voice as both passages take on the theme of the cyclic aspect of nature. A complete understanding of nature requires us to be fully aware of how important the cycles of nature are to us. An example of these is the sun's daily cycle, which brings us the light and darkness that are so prominent within the creation story of Genesis 1 and that give shape to our daily lives. Another example is the annual cycle of the seasons, as showcased by other entries in this anthology.

In addition to focusing on this cyclic aspect of nature, both passages also celebrate the sunrise. Their two authors employ the best powers of the literary imagination to capture the primeval and numinous quality of sunrise, which paradoxically is also commonplace by virtue of occurring every morning.

The poem within the entry, which is drawn from the first half of Psalm 19, can be divided into two distinct stanzas. The first directs our attention to the heavenly bodies in general. The poet compacts four important ideas into just eight lines: (1) that the heavenly bodies participate in a perpetual cycle from *day to day* and *night to night*; (2) that they are an artistic achievement that shows God's *handiwork*; (3) that they are a divine revelation that *reveals knowledge*; and (4) that this silent witness is universal—it goes *out through all the earth*.

William Trost Richards, *Lake Squam from Red Hill*, 1874

The focus of the second stanza then narrows specifically to the sun, which it pictures as dwelling in a *tent*—a metaphor for the sky that the preceding stanza has portrayed so evocatively. It employs two further metaphors to lend more punch to its rapturous celebration of the sun. The glory of the sunrise is compared to a man leaving his chamber on the most celebrative day of his life—a simile that carries over the excitement and visual splendor of a wedding day to the daily sunrise. The poem's theme about the cycles of nature then returns in the imagery of a runner exuberantly completing a race.

Mark Twain's passage about sunrise is one of the grandest passages in all American literature. It is so packed with imagery that it rises to the status of what literary scholars call prose poetry. The passage is part of an autobiographical account of the author's experience as a steamboat pilot on the Mississippi River. As Twain records the progress of a sunrise, he emphasizes its beauty. Three ingredients converge within the passage: the sights of sunrise, its sounds (which include silence), and the interior response of the person who is experiencing it. The result is a meditative landscape passage.

The edification of the passage is encapsulated in the speaker's receptivity to nature. Not only do we admire his attentiveness to all the details that the passage captures, but we also wish to be like him in his love of nature. We see that although the author has set out to capture the external beauty and splendor of the sunrise, these are only the means to something even more personally important—namely, the inner emotional effect of tranquility and peace that this beauty and splendor bring us. Although Twain does not push his description in a spiritual direction, a Christian reader automatically does so, by supplying a doxological awareness that God is the creator of the sunrise and that the beauty and tranquility of nature are his gifts to the human race.

We can follow the example set in these passages by drinking in the splendor of the sun's daily appearance and progress through the sky, while using this agent of nature of deepen our understanding of God as we relate to him. ■

A famous passage in Ecclesiastes encapsulates the core idea of this entry: "The sun rises, and the sun goes down, and hastens to the place where it rises" (1:5). To this we can add the Preacher's later declaration that "light is sweet, and it is pleasant for the eyes to see the sun" (11:7).

This Is My Father's World

Maltbie D. Babcock (1858–1901)

This is my Father's world,
And to my listening ears,
All nature sings, and around me rings
The music of the spheres.

This is my Father's world.
I rest me in the thought
Of rocks and trees, of skies and seas;
His hand the wonders wrought.

This is my Father's world.
The birds their carols raise,
The morning light, the lily white,
Declare their Maker's praise.

This is my Father's world.
He shines in all that's fair.
In the rustling grass I hear him pass.
He speaks to me everywhere.

This Is My Father's World

THE AUTHOR OF THIS NATURE HYMN was a talented and versatile man. He was a Presbyterian minister, a musician who played multiple instruments, an athlete who excelled in baseball and swimming, and an avid outdoorsman. He lived in Niagara County, New York, and would take regular walks on a lookout ridge that yielded views of farms, orchards, and Lake Ontario. As he would leave for these walks, Babcock's signature announcement was that he was "going out to see the Father's world." It is no wonder that this formula appears in the opening line of every stanza of the poem.

The first thing to note about this recurring line is that it is a declaration. It gives the poem the quality of a creed, a statement of belief that God owns the world in which we live. What does the poet mean by *world*? The hymn answers that question: for purposes of this poem, the *world* is the realm of physical nature.

The poet writes from the personal experience of a musician who is sensitive to sounds and of a hiker who has relished breathtaking landscape views. His testimony about God's world of nature accordingly combines both aural and visual imagery. Stanza 1 features sounds, and stanza 2 sights. Stanza 3 begins with two lines pertaining to sounds and then ends with two lines describing visual delights, and the final stanza employs the same principle of balancing halves, but with the order reversed.

The poem is an example of how the simple can serve as a form of beauty. Its thoughts and images are so straightforward that it is familiar in some circles as a children's song. Its simplicity is not inartistic, however; indeed, the verbal beauty of its lines lends them an aphoristic quality that makes them almost impossible to forget. The lines, in fact, are so well known that this hymn may rank as a cultural icon. As one evidence of this, the following aphorisms from the hymn have appeared within the titles of multiple books and music albums: *This is my father's world; all nature sings; he shines in all that's fair; he speaks to me everywhere.*

What about the poem as a work of nature writing? It employs the conventional nature-writing strategy of naming features of nature in a way that awakens our own experiences with and memories of them. The poet combines this strategy with a doctrinal agenda that leads him to declare that (a) God created the world, (b) the world of nature is a constant source of beauty and pleasure that is free for the taking, and (c) God speaks to us through this created beauty.

We can apply this poem by receiving its author's testimony as an invitation for us to experience nature as he does. Nature is beckoning, it tells us; and God is speaking. It is up to us whether to accept this invitation for us to see and hear. ■

Psalm 24:1–2 confirms this hymn's claim that God created and owns the world: "The earth is the Lord's and the fullness thereof, the world and those who dwell therein, for he has founded it."

previous: Thomas Moran, *Tower at Tower Falls, Yellowstone*, 1872
this page: Mansur, *Diving Dipper and Other Birds*, ca. 1535–45

Nature in Paradise

John Milton (1608–1674)

Nature as God Intended It

And higher than that wall a circling row
Of goodliest trees loaden with fairest fruit,
Blossoms and fruits at once of golden hue
Appeared, with gay enameled colors mixt:
On which the sun more glad impressed his beams
Than in fair evening cloud, or humid bow,
When God hath showered the earth; so lovely seemed
That landscape. . . . .

Beneath him with new wonder now he views
To all delight of human sense exposed
In narrow room Nature's whole wealth, yea more,
A heaven on earth, for blissful Paradise
Of God the garden was, by him in the East
Of Eden planted. . . . .

. . . . Nature here
Poured forth profuse on hill and dale and plain,
Both where the morning sun first warmly smote
The open field, and where the unpierced shade
Darkened the noontide bowers: thus was this place,
A happy rural seat of various view.

Nature in Paradise

Eve's Love Song to Adam

With thee conversing I forget all time;
All seasons and their change, all please alike.
Sweet is the breath of morn, her rising sweet,
With charm of earliest birds; pleasant the sun
When first on this delightful land he spreads
His orient beams, on herb, tree, fruit, and flower,
Glistering with dew; fragrant the fertile earth
After soft showers; and sweet the coming on
Of grateful evening mild, then silent night
With this her solemn bird and this fair moon,
And these the gems of heaven, her starry train.

Adam and Eve's Morning Hymn

Soon as they forth were come to open sight
Of dayspring, and the sun, who scarce up risen
With wheels yet hovering o'er the ocean brim,
Shot parallel to the earth his dewy ray,
Discovering in wide landscape all the east
Of Paradise and Eden's happy plains,
Lowly they bowed adoring, and began
Their orisons, each morning duly paid
In various style, for neither various style
Nor holy rapture wanted they to praise
Their Maker, in fit strains pronounced or sung,

. . . . and they thus began:
These are thy glorious works, Parent of good,
Almighty, thine this universal frame,
Thus wondrous fair; thyself how wondrous then!
Unspeakable, who sit above these heavens
To us invisible or dimly seen
In these thy lowest works, yet these declare
Thy goodness beyond thought, and power divine. ▪

Nature in Paradise

The term *Paradise is derived* from a Persian word for an enclosed royal garden. It most immediately evokes our sense of nature, though of course it also describes a state of spiritual perfection. And because the original Paradise was irrevocably lost, we further look on it as an object of nostalgia. Such nostalgia can lead to escapism or paralysis, but it can just as well be a part of psychic and emotional health. We need strong, positive images from the past to remind us that God did not create us to be weighed down by the misery that frequently surrounds us.

If Paradise is thus a memory, it is also an image of hope—an ideal toward which we can aspire, and one that we can sometimes attain, in our daily lives. Paradise is also an image of longing, and a leading purpose of literature is to awaken longing in us. The specific longing that Milton awakens through the passages of this entry is a longing for the beauty of nature. His descriptive technique helps to evoke this longing by giving us generalized pictures of nature that require us to fill in details using our own experience. If he had given us his own imagined picture of Paradise, C. S. Lewis points out that this would have distracted us "from the Paradisal idea as it exists in our [own] minds. . . . Yet Milton must *seem* to describe—you cannot just say nothing about Paradise in *Paradise Lost*. While seeming to describe his own imagination he must actually arouse ours."

With this understanding in place, we can readily make the passages of this entry our own. The first passage is our arrival in Paradise. Nearly every line within it introduces a new aspect of Paradise. The overall principle is that Paradise consists of whatever we human beings find to be the best and most beautiful aspects of nature. The second passage contains part of a love poem that Eve addresses to Adam. Its lines also awaken our love and longing for nature in its ideal forms and evoke the experiences we ourselves have had with nature, from sunrise to nightfall, that we treasure most. The third passage keeps the evocative images of nature flowing, but it adds an element of worship to them as well. Nature itself provides the substance of Adam and Eve's song of praise to God.

Other entries in this anthology put us in touch with nature as we know it in the world around us, but these paradisal passages lift us to another realm. They show us not simply nature as we know it but nature as God intended it. We can apply these lines from Milton to our own experience by doing what C. S. Lewis commends—namely, to "find again in our own depth the Paradisal light" and to allow it to inspire us to love nature and worship God in the process. ∎

The text on which Milton built his picture of the garden of Eden is Genesis 2:8–9: "And the Lord God planted a garden in Eden, in the east, and there he put the man whom he had formed. And out of the ground the Lord God made to spring up every tree that is pleasant to the sight and good for food."

previous: Fan (French), 1700s
this page: *Stylized Landscape*, ca. 1850–1899

The Beauty of the World

Jonathan Edwards (1703–1758)

The beauty of the world consists wholly of sweet mutual connections, either within itself or with the supreme being. As to the physical world, though there are many other sorts of connections, yet the sweetest and most charming beauty of it is its resemblance of spiritual beauties. The reason is that spiritual beauties are infinitely the greatest, and bodies being but the shadows of beings, they must be so much the more charming as they shadow forth spiritual beauties. This beauty is peculiar to natural things, surpassing the art of man....

    The wonderful suitableness of green for the grass and plants, the blues of the sky, the white of the clouds, the colors of flowers, consists in a complicated proportion that these colors make one with another.... There is a great suitableness between the objects of different senses, as between sounds, colors, and smells; as between colors of the woods and flowers and their smells and the singing of birds.... The gentle motions of waves and of the lily are agreeable to other things that represent calmness, gentleness, and benevolence; the fields and woods seem to rejoice, and how joyful do the birds seem to be in it. How much resemblance is there of every grace in the field covered with plants and flowers when the sun shines serenely and undisturbedly upon them, what a resemblance, I say, of every grace and beautiful disposition of mind. . . . How great a resemblance of a holy and virtuous soul is a calm, serene day. . . .

There are beauties that are more palpable and explicable, and there are hidden and secret beauties. The former pleases, and we can tell why. . . . The latter sort are those beauties that delight us, and we cannot tell why. Thus we find ourselves pleased in beholding the color of the violets, but we know not what secret regularity or harmony it is that creates that pleasure in our minds. These hidden beauties are commonly by far the greatest, because the more complex a beauty is, the more hidden is it. In this latter fact consists principally the beauty of the world, and very much in light and colors. Thus mere light is pleasing to the mind. . . . How lovely is the green of the face of the earth in all manner of colors, in flowers, the color of the skies, and lovely tinctures of the morning and evening. ■

T<small>HIS PASSAGE, WHICH IS FROM A BRIEF TREATISE</small> by Jonathan Edwards, contains nearly every ingredient that we expect in nature writing. At the base of nature writing is the author's enthusiasm for nature. We intuitively experience a nature writer as a kindred spirit and readily embrace him or her as a model whom we want to emulate. In addition, we unconsciously receive the author's assertions about nature as credible.

The excitement about nature that Jonathan Edwards displays in this passage is everywhere a hallmark of his writing. In his famous *Personal*

previous: Francis Seymour Haden, *An Early Riser*, 1897
this page: Vilhelm Hammershøi, *Moonlight, Strandgade 30*, 1900–6

Narrative, Edwards recounts how his rapture over nature exploded after his conversion: "The appearance of everything was altered. . . . God's excellency, his wisdom, his purity and love, seemed to appear in everything; in the sun, moon and stars; in the clouds, and blue sky; in the grass, flowers, trees; in the water, and all nature; which used greatly to fix my mind. I often used to sit and view the moon, for a long time; and so in the daytime, spent much time in viewing the clouds and sky, to behold the sweet glory of God in these things."

The specific focus of the nature passage within this entry is on its beauty—a focus that is also strongly associated with Edwards. Edwards possessed the imagination of an artist as well as the reasoning of a theologian. In this passage, his artist's love of the beauty of nature finds expression in his description of its visual effects. Reading his descriptions is like looking at a painting by an impressionist such as Monet.

And the passage combines his observation with analysis—which allows a particular theory regarding nature, one associated with Edwards, to shine through. When Edwards looked at nature, what he primarily saw was an interconnectedness of diverse parts. On a purely natural plane, such connections exist among the colors and motions and sounds of nature working together to produce harmony. But Edwards's theory about the connections between earthly and divine beauty is even better known. He wrote a whole treatise titled *Images or Shadows of Divine Things*, which proposes that the beauties of nature are shadows of heavenly realities—and preeminently of the attributes of God.

This passage combines the three qualities we most associate with nature writing: an infectious excitement over nature by an author who loves it, an awakening of our own awareness of the beauty of nature that exists around us, and encouragement for us to develop a well-thought-out set of ideas about nature. We can apply the passage by allowing it to perform these three functions for us.

Jonathan Edwards's theory that the diverse forms of nature all have their special beauty aligns with Paul's writings in 1 Corinthians 15:40–41: "There are heavenly bodies and earthly bodies, but the glory of the heavenly is of one kind, and the glory of the earthly is of another. There is one glory of the sun, and another glory of the moon, and another glory of the stars."

Let Them Praise the Name of the Lord

Psalm 148

Praise the Lord!
Praise the Lord from the heavens;
 praise him in the heights!
Praise him, all his angels;
 praise him, all his hosts!

Praise him, sun and moon,
 praise him, all you shining stars!
Praise him, you highest heavens,
 and you waters above the heavens!

Let them praise the name of the Lord!
 For he commanded and they were created.
And he established them forever and ever;
 he gave a decree, and it shall not pass away.

Praise the Lord from the earth,
 you great sea creatures and all deeps,
fire and hail, snow and mist,
 stormy wind fulfilling his word!

Mountains and all hills,
    fruit trees and all cedars!
Beasts and all livestock,
    creeping things and flying birds!

Kings of the earth and all peoples,
    princes and all rulers of the earth!
Young men and maidens together,
    old men and children!

Let them praise the name of the Lord,
    for his name alone is exalted;
    his majesty is above earth and heaven.

He has raised up a horn for his people,
    praise for all his saints,
    for the people of Israel who are near to him.
Praise the Lord!

Let Them Praise the Name of the Lord

PSALM 148 IS ONE OF A KIND. As one tribute to its uniqueness, it is probably the most paraphrased psalm behind Psalm 23. John Milton followed its structure and content when he composed Adam and Eve's morning hymn in *Paradise Lost*, and literary author Joseph Addison based a famous hymn on it ("The Spacious Firmament on High"). How might we account for the psalm's appeal to poets and hymnwriters?

Although most nature writing tends toward a descriptive-meditative mode, Psalm 148 is a fireworks poem. It does not primarily describe nature, or meditate on it, but instead expresses excitement over it. The technique the poet uses to express this excitement is a figure of speech called apostrophe ("direct address")—in fact, this poem is mainly a catalog of apostrophes. Because apostrophe is an understood way of expressing strong feeling, the string of apostrophes we find in Psalm 148 not only expresses excitement but elicits it from us as we read.

The specific apostrophes within this psalm are commands to praise God, and this brings a second literary form into play. The technical term for a command to praise God is a *doxology*.

The structure of Psalm 148 is part of its artistry and appeal. Its commands to praise God move down the scale of nature. The poet begins with the heavenly bodies, which include the angels, and then shifts his focus downward to *the earth* to include the animals and plants. Then, in a surprise move, he places people into the order of nature and commands them to join their fellow creatures in this chorus. Twice, these commands to praise God are interrupted by stanzas that offer a reason for doing so. These stanzas begin with the formula *Let them praise the name of the Lord, for* . . . The second of them is extended in order to make the point that people have a reason for praising God in addition to their status as his creatures—namely, their salvation. A final pleasing touch that the poem's organization provides is its envelope structure; the repetition, at the very end, of its opening line provides a quiet resting point after the high voltage of the content that has preceded it.

We can apply the poem by entering into its spirit of celebration and by registering the point that the nature we celebrate encompasses the entire cosmos. Our enthusiasm for nature should extend to more than our own backyards—it should include the entire social order. ■

The signature feature of Psalm 148 is the way it exuberantly portrays the forces of nature celebrating a grand event as people do at a festival. Nature poets elsewhere in the Bible use the same technique. An example is Isaiah 55:12: "The mountains and the hills . . . shall break forth into singing, and all the trees of the field shall clap their hands."

previous: Joseph Mallord William Turner, *The Lake of Zug*, 1843
this page: Abbott Handerson Thayer, *Mount Monadnock*, ca. 1911/1914

Pierre Joseph Redouté, *Pink Roses in a Vase*, 1838

Notes

Most of the external facts that are attached to the poems in this anthology belong to a common storehouse. This information appears in numerous sources, both print and electronic, making it misleading to attach it to a specific source. Whenever information for a given entry is tied to a specific source, or when I judged that a reader might want further details, I have provided a note.

Many of the texts that are used for the literary readings have been lightly edited or modernized.

The **introduction** alludes to the book by Simon Martin, Martin Butlin, and Robert Meyrick, *Poets in the Landscape: The Romantic Spirit in British Art* (Chichester, UK: Pallant House Gallery, 2007). John Milton's claim that Christian poetry has the ability "to set the affections in right tune" appears in his treatise *Reason of Church Government Urged against Prelaty*, widely available in editions of Milton's works and from web sources.

In the commentary on **Psalm 65:5–13**, the quotations from C. S. Lewis are taken from *Reflections on the Psalms* (London: Geoffrey Bles, 1958), 77.

The entry from Martin Luther on **God's presence in nature** is a conflation of passages from volumes 37, 5, 51, and 54 of *Luther's Works*, respectively. The individual volumes are as follows: Martin Luther, "That These Words of Christ, 'This Is My Body,' etc., Still Stand Firm against the Fanatics," 1527, trans. Robert H. Fischer, in *Word and Sacrament III*, ed. Robert H. Fischer, Luther's Works 37 (Philadelphia: Muhlenberg Press, 1961), 57–58, 60–61; Martin Luther, *Lectures on Genesis: Chapters 26–30*, ed.

Notes

Jaroslav Pelikan, trans. George V. Schick and Paul D. Pahl, Luther's Works 5 (St. Louis, Concordia Publishing House, 1968), 197; Martin Luther, *Sermons I*, ed. and trans. John W. Doberstein, Luther's Works 51 (Philadelphia: Muhlenberg Press, 1959), 43; Martin Luther, *Table Talk*, ed. and trans. Theodore G. Tappert, Luther's Works 54 (Philadelphia: Fortress Press, 1967), 327, 351. The quotation from *Table Talk* in the commentary comes Martin Luther, quoted in *The Life of Luther: Written by Himself*, ed. Jules Michelet, trans. William Hazlitt (London, 1846), 266.

The entry here titled **"Canticle of the Creatures"** is shortened from the Italian original as translated by Benen Fahy in the following source: *St. Francis of Assisi: Writings and Early Biographies*, ed. Marion A. Habig, 3rd rev. ed. (Chicago: Franciscan Herald Press, 1973), 130–31.

The entry from the **Book of Common Prayer** is a collection of passages from multiple places in multiple editions of the Prayerbook, edited to make a coherent set of prayers about nature.

The entry by John Calvin about the **theater of God's glory** consists of excerpts from *Institutes of the Christian Religion*, trans. John Allen, 6th American ed., vol. 1 (Philadelphia, 1813), 1.5.5; 1.6.2; 1.14.20; 1.14.21; 3.10.2.

Henry Van Dyke's claim about the inspiration for his hymn

Facsimile of painted ceiling (Egypt), ca. 1390–1352 BC

"Joyful, Joyful We Adore Thee" is related by his son in Tertius Van Dyke, "Joyful, Joyful, We Adore Thee," in *The Music of the Gospel*, ed. Stanley Armstrong Hunter (New York: Abingdon Press, 1932), 25; and his son's quotation is from Tertius Van Dyke, *Henry Van Dyke: A Biography* (New York: Harper & Brothers, 1935), 24–25.

The title for Wordsworth's **sunrise sonnet**, as originally published, highlights its factual basis: "Composed upon Westminster Bridge, September 3, 1802." That wording does not mean that Wordsworth composed the poem as he sat on the bridge but instead means he composed it *about*, or *on the subject of*, Westminster Bridge—along with what he saw from it. Lines have been omitted from the sunset sonnet because they are extraneous to its nature focus.

In the compilation on **where beauty can be found**, the Edgar Allan Poe passage is taken from Edgar Allan Poe, "The Poetic Principle," found in *The Works of the Late Edgar Allan Poe: With Notices of His Life and Genius*, vol. 3, *The Literati: Some Honest Opinions about Autorial Merits and Demerits, with Occasional Words of Personality, Together with Marginalia, Suggestions, and Essays*, ed. Rufus Wilmot Griswold (New York, 1850), 19. The possibility of Poe's conversion is elaborated in Harry Lee Poe, *Evermore: Edgar Allan Poe and the Mystery of the Universe* (Waco: Baylor University Press, 2012), 165–76. The first two paragraphs by Jonathan Edwards are taken from Jonathan Edwards, *Observations Concerning the Scripture Œconomy of the Trinity and Covenant of Redemption* (New York, 1880), 94–95. His third paragraph is taken from Jonathan Edwards, "The Nature of True Virtue," in *Two Dissertations* (Boston, 1765), 126. The quotation from Psalm 90 on page 57 incorporates alternate wording from a footnote within the ESV.

In the commentary on Keats's poem **"To Autumn,"** the quote from C. S. Lewis is from *English Literature in the Sixteenth Century* (Oxford: Clarendon Press, 1954), 26.

The sources in the compilation about nature being a **revelation from God** are as follows: The passage from Thomas Shepherd appears in *The Sincere Convert* (Cambridge, 1664), 2–3. The Thomas Taylor excerpt comes from "Meditations from the Creatures," found in *A Man in Christ, or A New Creature* (London, 1635), 23. Richard Baxter is quoted from "The Catechising of Families," 1682, reprinted in *The Practical Works of the Rev. Richard Baxter*, ed. William Orme (London, 1830), 19:129.

Notes

The passages that comprise the selection on **nature as an aid to understanding godliness** are taken from the Bible in the following sequence: Psalms 1:3; 52:8; 92:12–14; 125:1–2; 128:1, 3; and Proverbs 4:18.

In the selection about **epiphany in nature**, the passage from *Great Expectations* occurs in Charles Dickens, *Great Expectations*, chapter 58, in *All the Year Round* 5, no. 119 (1861): 433. The anecdote involving Tennyson was originally published in *The Times*, 13 October 1892, and then reprinted in R. E. Welsh, "Homage to Christ from Modern Magi: Quotations from the Great Writers," in *The Puritan: An Illustrated Magazine for Free Churchmen*, vols. 1–2 (London, 1899), 222. Wordsworth's comments about spots of time appear in Book 12 of his long autobiographical poem *The Prelude*. C. S. Lewis's claim that the particulars of literature are a net whereby to capture the universal appears in his essay "On Stories," in *Essays Presented to Charles Williams*, ed. C. S. Lewis (1947; repr., Grand Rapids: William B. Eerdmans, 1966), 103.

Mary Lathbury's **"Day Is Dying in the West,"** as originally composed, consisted of the first two stanzas that are well known. Singers felt that this was too brief, so in 1890 Lathbury added the remaining two stanzas. A refrain that was incorporated later, based on a traditional chorus titled "Sanctus," adds a praise element but dilutes the effect of the original. Christopher R. Miller is the author of *The Invention of Evening: Perception and Time in Romantic Poetry* (Cambridge: Cambridge University Press, 2006).

Portions of the Ralph Waldo Emerson entry about **nature always changing** appear in his essay "The American Scholar," published as *An Oration Delivered before the Phi Beta Kappa Society, at Cambridge, August 31, 1837*, 2nd. ed. (Boston, 1838), 6, while the rest is taken from Ralph Waldo Emerson, *Nature* (Boston, 1836), 12, 21, 23, 24.

In the entry regarding **walking in nature**, Jonathan Edwards's *Personal Narrative* is a brief autobiography that he wrote sometime around 1739. It was published posthumously in 1765.

The entry by Nathaniel Hawthorne, regarding **God's blessing us through nature**, consists of excerpts taken from *Passages from the American Notebooks of Nathaniel Hawthorne*, ed. Sophia Hawthorne (1868; repr., Boston, 1883), 218, 355, 357.

The quotation from Samuel Taylor Coleridge that accompanies **"The

Snow Storm" commentary is taken from his literary biography titled *Biographia Literaria; or Biographical Sketches of My Literary Life and Opinions* (London, 1817), 1:85, italics added.

In the entry on the **archetypal river**, the specific literary works excerpted are as follows: William Wordsworth, "Remembrance of Collins"; Charles Dickens, *Great Expectations*, chapter 15, in *All the Year Round* 4, no. 92 (1861): 362; Kenneth Grahame, *The Wind in the Willows* (New York: Charles Scribner's Sons, 1908), 4. The suggestion that a river figures prominently in the lives of most people comes from Norm Bomer, *Sons of the River: A Nebraska Memoir* (Moscow, ID: Canon Press, 2000), 13.

"**Lessons from Nature**" was printed as part of C. H. Spurgeon, *The Metropolitan Tabernacle Pulpit: Sermons Preached and Revised*, vol. 17 (London, 1872), 445–47.

The **devotional insights of George Washington Carver** have been preserved for posterity within his letters, and this anthology's passage about communing with God through nature is a collage of gleanings from those

Caspar David Friedrich, *Northern Landscape, Spring*, ca. 1825

Notes

letters. Those letters, as well as the quoted material in their commentary, are available in *George Washington Carver in His Own Words*, ed. Gary R. Kremer (Columbia, MO: University of Missouri Press, 1987), 138, 141–43—specifically the chapter titled "The Scientist as Mystic: Reading God out of Nature's Book." Reprinted with the permission of University of Missouri Press.

In the entry on **the house that God built and furnished**, the passage from Martin Luther appears in *Luther on the Creation: A Critical and Devotional Commentary on Genesis*, ed. and trans. John Nicholas Lenker (Minneapolis: Lutherans in All Lands, 1904), 80, 84–85, as part of his commentary on Genesis 1:10–11. "Caedmon's Hymn," which was originally written in Old English, has been translated by the editor for this anthology. The story about Caedmon comes from the Venerable Bede's *Ecclesiastical History of England*, which is widely available in print and web formats.

The passage from Mark Twain within the entry about a **bridegroom leaving his chamber** is from his *Life on the Mississippi* (Boston, 1883), 331–32.

The passages from *Paradise Lost* can be found in the following places within Milton's epic: book 4, lines 146–53, 205–210, 242–47, 639–49; book 5, lines 138–48, 152–59. The quotations from C. S. Lewis are from *A Preface to Paradise Lost* (New York: Oxford University Press, 1942), 47.

Alexandre Calame, *Fallen Tree*, 1839/1845

Image Credits

ALL ARTWORKS IN THIS BOOK have been reproduced in good faith, recognizing copyrights where required. Many images have been cropped to fit the format of this book.

Special thanks are due to the following museums for providing artwork and helpful information: Art Institute of Chicago, Barnes Foundation (Philadelphia), Detroit Institute of Arts, Metropolitan Museum of Art (New York), National Gallery of Art (Washington, DC), National Library of Wales (Aberystwyth), Philadelphia Museum of Art, and Toledo Museum of Art.

5 Vincent van Gogh, *Oleanders*, ca. 1888, oil on canvas, Metropolitan Museum of Art, www.metmuseum.org.

6–7 *Birds*, ca. 1840, oil on canvas, National Gallery of Art, www.nga.gov.

8, 9 Dish with rocks, flowers, and birds, 1710–30, hard-paste porcelain with colored enamels under transparent glaze, Metropolitan Museum of Art.

10–11 Léon Richet, *The Spring*, 1882, oil on panel, Philadelphia Museum of Art, www.philamuseum.org.

12 Joris Hoefnagel, *Plate 13: A Tiger, a Lynx, and a Jaguar(?)*, ca. 1575/1580, watercolor and gouache, with oval border in gold, on vellum, National Gallery of Art.

13 Joris Hoefnagel, *Plate 33: A Pair of Bohemian Waxwings, a Shelduck(?), and a Brant Goose with a Ginger Plant*, ca. 1575/1580, watercolor and gouache, with oval border in gold, on vellum, National Gallery of Art.

14 William Turner of Oxford, *Dawn in the Valley*, 1832, watercolor with scratching out and gum arabic on wove paper, National Gallery of Art.

17 Jean-François Millet, *Haystacks: Autumn*, ca. 1874, oil on canvas, Metropolitan Museum of Art.

18–19   Karl Gaff, *Canadian Pond Weed Leaf Tip*, 2021, focus stack captured in compensated polarized light microscopy (magnification x100), CC BY 4.0. https://creativecommons.org/licenses/by-sa/4.0/deed.en.

20   John La Farge, *Nocturne*, ca. 1885, watercolor, gouache, and charcoal on off-white wove paper adhered to wove paper, Metropolitan Museum of Art.

29   Netsuke of bird on her nest, 1800s, ivory, Metropolitan Museum of Art.

22   Gerhard Emmoser, Celestial globe with clockwork, 1579, partially gilded silver, gilded brass, brass, steel, Metropolitan Museum of Art.

24   Jean-Baptiste-Camille Corot, *The Eel Gatherers*, 1860/1865, oil on canvas, National Gallery of Art.

25   Joseph Mallord William Turner, *Keelmen Heaving in Coals by Moonlight*, 1835, oil on canvas, National Gallery of Art.

27   Richard Wilson, *Lake Albano*, 1762, oil on canvas, National Gallery of Art.

29   Deepak Sundar, *European Robin Looks*, 2019, photograph, https://www.instagram.com/p/B40Fou0IcoG/, CC BY-SA 4.0, https://creativecommons.org/licenses/by-sa/4.0/.

31   Rembrandt Peale, *Rubens Peale with a Geranium*, 1801, oil on canvas, National Gallery of Art.

35   Camille Corot, *The Ferryman*, ca. 1865, oil on canvas, Metropolitan Museum of Art.

36–37   Severin Roesen, *Still Life: Flowers and Fruit*, 1850–55, oil on canvas, Metropolitan Museum of Art.

38–39   Camille Pissarro, *The Artist's Garden at Eragny*, 1898, oil on canvas, National Gallery of Art.

40   John Brett, *Kynance*, 1888, oil on canvas, Metropolitan Museum of Art.

42   Joseph Rodefer DeCamp, *The Seamstress*, 1916, oil on canvas, National Gallery of Art.

44–45   Worthington Whittredge, *Second Beach, Newport*, 1865, oil on canvas, Philadelphia Museum of Art.

46, 47   Coat, 1775–85, silk, Metropolitan Museum of Art.

49   Joseph Bartholomew Kidd, *Sharp-Tailed Finch*, 1831/1833, pencil and oil on millboard, National Gallery of Art.

50–51   Nikodem Nijaki, *Rhododendron smirnowii blossom IMGP3243*, 2011, photograph, CC BY-SA 3.0, https://creativecommons.org/licenses/by-sa/3.0/.

52–53   Mark Catesby, *Rhododendron*, 1731–54, hand-colored etching and engraving, Philadelphia Museum of Art.

56   Wilhelm Amberg, *Young Woman Seated by a Stream (Contemplation)*, before 1886, oil on canvas, Philadelphia Museum of Art.

59   Nicolaes Maes, *Young Woman Peeling Apples*, ca. 1655, oil on wood, Metropolitan Museum of Art.

60–61   Jean-François Millet, *Autumn Landscape with a Flock of Turkeys*, 1872–73, oil on canvas, Metropolitan Museum of Art.

62–63   John William Casilear, *Lake George*, after 1851, oil on canvas, National Gallery of Art.

64   Joris Hoefnagel, *Hairy Dragonfly and Two Darters*, ca. 1575/1580, watercolor and gouache, with oval border in gold, on vellum, National Gallery of Art.

65   Joris Hoefnagel, *Plate 33: Moth and Butterfly with Other Insects and a Columbine Flower*, ca. 1575/1580, watercolor and gouache, with oval border in gold, on vellum, National Gallery of Art.

66–67   John Singer Sargent, *Olive Trees, Corfu*, 1909, watercolor and opaque watercolor with scraping and wax resist over graphite on ivory wove paper, Art Institute of Chicago, www.artic.edu.

68–69   William Trost Richards, *Beach at Long Branch: Sunrise*, 1872, oil on canvas, Detroit Institute of Arts, www.dia.org.

70–71   Irving Ramsey Wiles, *Spring Woods*, ca. 1900–20, oil on panel, Philadelphia Museum of Art.

72   William Langson Lathrop, *Spring Landscape*, ca. 1915, oil on canvas, Philadelphia Museum of Art.

73, 75   Jan van Kessel the Elder, *Vanitas Still Life*, ca. 1665/1670, oil on copper, National Gallery of Art.

78–79   John Frederick Kensett, *October in the Marshes*, 1872, oil on canvas, National Gallery of Art.

80–81   Washington Allston, *A Landscape after Sunset*, ca. 1819, oil on canvas, National Gallery of Art.

83   Théodore Rousseau, *Sunset near Arbonne*, ca. 1860–65, oil on wood, Metropolitan Museum of Art.

86–87   Friedrich Salathé, *Rays of Sunlight Striking a Woodland Path*, ca. 1815, watercolor with pen and black ink over graphite on wove paper, National Gallery of Art.

88–91   Joseph Pennell, *Kensington Gardens*, 1887, etching, Philadelphia Museum of Art.

90–91   Henri-Edmond Cross, *Landscape*, ca. 1904, watercolor and crayon on paper, Metropolitan Museum of Art.

92–93   Thomas Gainsborough, *Landscape with Rustic Lovers, Two Cows, and a Man on a Distant Bridge*, ca. 1755–59, oil on canvas, Philadelphia Museum of Art.

Image Credits

- 94 John Callcott Horsley, *Lovers under a Blossom Tree*, by 1859, oil on canvas, Philadelphia Museum of Art.
- 96 Suzuki Harunobu, *Birds and Narcissus*, ca. 1615–1868, woodblock print; ink and color on paper, Metropolitan Museum of Art.
- 98 Zhu Ling, *Black Cat and Narcissus*, 1800s, hanging scroll; ink and color on paper, Metropolitan Museum of Art.
- 100–1 Thomas Chambers, *The Connecticut Valley*, mid 1800s, oil on canvas, National Gallery of Art.
- 102 Henry Golden Dearth, *Flecks of Foam*, ca. 1911/1912, oil on wood, National Gallery of Art.
- 105 J. Ashford, *Tintern Abbey*, 1820, oil on board, Llyfrgell Genedlaethol Cymru / The National Library of Wales, www.artuk.org.
- 106 John "Warwick" Smith, *Tintern Abbey by Moonlight*, ca. 1789, graphite and watercolor with scratching out, Metropolitan Museum of Art.
- 108 Tom Ek, *Winter Forest after Snow Storm*, 2018, digital photograph, www.commons.wikimedia.org, CC BY-SA 2.0, https://creativecommons.org/licenses/by-sa/2.0/.
- 110–11 Eugène Isabe, *A Storm off the Normandy Coast*, probably 1850s, oil on paper, laid down on canvas, Metropolitan Museum of Art.
- 113 *Job*, 1618/30, oil on canvas, Art Institute of Chicago.
- 115, 117 Frits Thaulow, *Picquigny*, 1899, oil on canvas, Metropolitan Museum of Art.
- 120 Georges Seurat, *The Forest at Pontaubert*, 1881, oil on canvas, Metropolitan Museum of Art.
- 122 Sam Ferrara, *Matterhorn Sunset*, 2016, digital photograph, www.commons wikimedia.org, CC0 1.0, https://creativecommons.org/publicdomain/zero/1.0/.
- 125 Anton Dieffenbach, *Window*, 1856, oil on paper, laid down on canvas, Metropolitan Museum of Art.
- 126–28 Box for inkstone and writing implements (suzuri-bako) with geese against Mount Fuji in moonlight and (inner lid) with plovers by the seashore, early to mid-1800s, black lacquer ground with gold and silver maki-e, Metropolitan Museum of Art.
- 129 Attributed to Dierick Bouts the Elder, *Moses and the Burning Bush, with Moses Removing His Shoes*, ca. 1465–70, oil on panel, Metropolitan Museum of Art.
- 130 Nose ornament with shrimp, 500–600s, gold, silver, stone, Metropolitan Museum of Art.

130, 134 Gilt terracotta statuette of a goat, 1300s BC, terracotta, gold, Metropolitan Museum of Art.

130, 134 Miniature camelid effigy, 1400–1535, alloys of silver, gold and copper, Metropolitan Museum of Art.

130 Animal pendant, ca. 1–1000, gold, Metropolitan Museum of Art.

130, 134 Furniture plaque: wing of a hawk, ca. 1700s BC, ivory (hippopotamus), Metropolitan Museum of Art.

130 Lion (one of a pair), ca. 1732, hard-paste porcelain, Metropolitan Museum of Art.

130, 134 Tuning key for a zither, 200s BC, bronze, Metropolitan Museum of Art.

130, 134 Textile ornament, 1300–1400s, silver, Metropolitan Museum of Art.

130 Attributed to Hon'ami Kōetsu, writing box (suzuri-bako) with design of a deer, 1600s, lacquer on wood with lead and mother-of-pearl inlay, Philadelphia Museum of Art.

131, 134 Birdstone, 1500–500 BC, slate, Metropolitan Museum of Art.

131 Vessel terminating in the forepart of a bull, ca. 1300–1200s BC, silver, Metropolitan Museum of Art.

131, 134 Toad, possibly 1500s, bronze, Metropolitan Museum of Art.

131 Leaf bead, ca. 1390–1352 BC, faience, Metropolitan Museum of Art.

131, 134 Terracotta zoomorphic askos (vessel), 1900–1600 BC, terracotta; white painted ware, Metropolitan Museum of Art.

131, 134 Animal figurine, ca. 1981–1640 BC, clay, Metropolitan Museum of Art.

131, 134 Cosmetic vessel in the shape of a cat, ca. 1990–1900 BC, travertine (Egyptian alabaster), copper, quartz crystal, paint, Metropolitan Museum of Art.

previous: Edgar Degas, *Landscape*, 1892
this page: Emil Ganso, *Stream with Bridge and Lamp*, 1916

135–37 Izaak van Oosten, *The Garden of Eden*, 1658/1660, oil on canvas, Toledo Museum of Art, www.commons.wikimedia.org.

139 Charles Sheeler, *Home, Sweet Home*, 1931, oil on canvas, Detroit Institute of Arts.

140–41 Martin Johnson Heade, *Hummingbird and Apple Blossoms*, 1875, oil on canvas, Metropolitan Museum of Art.

142 George Inness, *Spring Blossoms, Montclair, New Jersey*, ca. 1891, oil and crayon or charcoal on canvas, Metropolitan Museum of Art.

Henri-Joseph Harpignies, Landscape, 1898

Image Credits

143, 145 John Martin, *Lake Squam from Red Hill*, 1847, watercolor, gouache, and graphite on light gray-green wove paper, Metropolitan Museum of Art.

147 Thomas Moran, *Tower at Tower Falls, Yellowstone*, 1872, watercolor and gouache over graphite on blue laid paper, National Gallery of Art.

148 Mansur, *Diving Dipper and Other Birds*, Folio from the Shah Jahan Album, ca. 1535–45, ink, opaque watercolor, and gold on paper, Metropolitan Museum of Art.

150–51 Fan, 1700s, ivory, gold, silver, Metropolitan Museum of Art.

153 *Stylized Landscape*, ca. 1850–1899, oil on canvas, National Gallery of Art.

154–55 Francis Seymour Haden, *An Early Riser*, 1897, mezzotint (with etching?) in green, National Gallery of Art.

156 Vilhelm Hammershøi, *Moonlight, Strandgade 30*, 1900–1906, oil on canvas, Metropolitan Museum of Art.

158, 159 Joseph Mallord William Turner, *The Lake of Zug*, 1843, watercolor over graphite, Metropolitan Museum of Art.

160–61 Abbott Handerson Thayer, *Mount Monadnock*, ca. 1911/1914, oil on canvas, National Gallery of Art.

162 Attributed to Pierre Joseph Redouté, *Pink Roses in a Vase*, 1838, watercolor and gouache over graphite on vellum, National Gallery of Art.

164 William J. Palmer-Jones, Facsimile of painted ceiling, ca. 1390–1352 BC, tempera on paper, Metropolitan Museum of Art.

167 Caspar David Friedrich, *Northern Landscape, Spring*, ca. 1825, oil on canvas, National Gallery of Art.

168 Alexandre Calame, *Fallen Tree*, 1839/1845, oil on paper on canvas, National Gallery of Art.

170–71 Edgar Degas, *Landscape*, 1892, monotype in oil colors, heightened with pastel, National Gallery of Art.

173 Emil Ganso, *Stream with Bridge and Lamp*, 1916, watercolor on off-white wove paper, Philadelphia Museum of Art.

175 Henri-Joseph Harpignies, *Landscape*, 1898, oil on canvas, National Gallery of Art.

176 Jean Bourdichon, *The Pentecost*, ca. 1480, tempera, granular gold paint, inscribed brown ink, pen and ink, and gilding on parchment, Barnes Foundation, www.collection.barnesfoundation.org.

Scripture Index

Genesis
1—121, 138, 145
1:1—139
1:2—128
1:31—107
2:8-9—153
24:63-65—95

Exodus
3:5—129

1 Chronicles
29:11—103

Job
12:7-8—30
12:10—30
28—56
38:22—109
40:4—79
40:8—112
42:5—42

Psalms
19:1-2—39
19:2—65
19:4—65
24:1-2—149
42:8—83

46:4—117
65:8—45
67:6—60
90:1—98
90:3—98
90:5-6—98
90:12—98
90:17—57
95:4-5—113
104:17-18—122
105:2—27
118:24—142
125:1—86
147:16—12
147:17—108
148—23, 160

Ecclesiastes
1:5—146
3:11—53
7:29—72
11:7—146

Isaiah
6:3—134
42:5—101
43:19—87
55:12—24, 161

Matthew
6:28—91
6:31—91

Luke
12:6-7—49
19:44—17

John
7:38—69

Romans
1:20—125

1 Corinthians
1:26-28—53
15:40-41—157

Colossians
1:16-17—21

1 Timothy
4:4-5—35

1 John
2:17—75

Revelation
22—121

Jean Bourdichon, *The Pentecost*, ca. 1480